MASTERING THE COMPUTER FOR DESIGN AND ILLUSTRATION

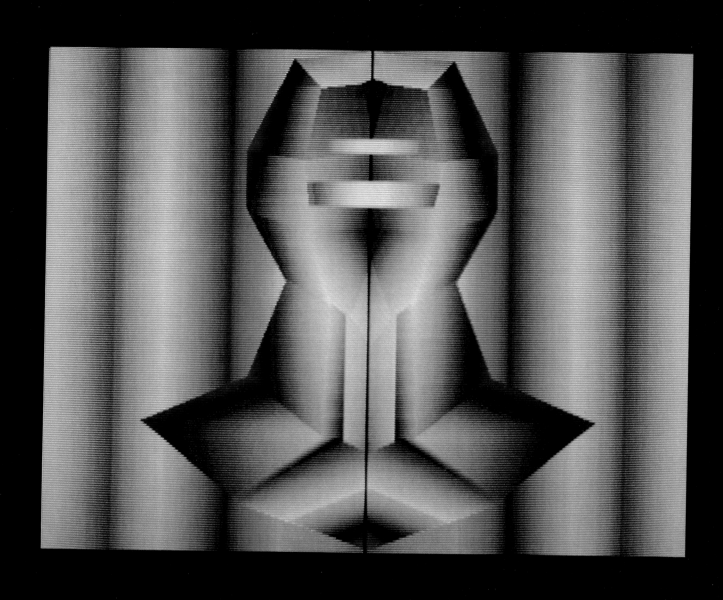

MASTERING THE COMPUTER FOR DESIGN AND ILLUSTRATION

DON BOLOGNESE

COLUMBUS BOOKS
LONDON

To my partner, Elaine Raphael, who deserves the credit for initiating the proposal that led to this book, especially its main purpose: to speak directly and without technical jargon to our friends, colleagues, and fellow artists in the field of graphic design.

Copyright © 1988 Don Bolognese

First published in 1988 in New York
by Watson-Guptill Publications,
a division of Billboard Publications, Inc.,
1515 Broadway, New York, NY 10036.

First published in Great Britain in 1988
by Columbus Books Limited of
19-23 Ludgate Hill, London EC4M 7PD.

British Library Cataloguing-in-Publication Data
Bolognese, Don
  Mastering the computer for design and illustration.

  1. Design. Applications of computer systems
  I. Title
  745.4′028′5

ISBN 0-86287-432-7

Manufactured in the United States of America

First printing, 1988

1 2 3 4 5 6 7 8 9/93 92 91 90 89 88

ACKNOWLEDGMENTS

As I've said a number of times in a vain quest for sympathy (from friends, editors, and clients)—doing a book on computer graphics at the desktop level is like trying to hit a moving and changing target while riding backwards on a galloping horse. Now it's done, and I wish to thank those people who kept me on target (and on the horse) with encouragement and pertinent, up-to-date information, plus some well-informed guesses about future trends in the industry, especially those that promise exciting challenges for artists.

For enlightening interviews about computer graphics in the TV area, my thanks to Robert Brandel and Ralph Famiglietta, Jr., of NBC News, and Jenny Choi, one of NBC's paintbox artists. For a broad overview of the state of computer graphics in print and video and some specific glimpses into the not-too-distant future, my thanks to Dean Ross Eaker, editor and publisher of *Computer Pictures* magazine. And many thanks to that publication for permission to use some of the material on comps and finished art that first appeared in their January-February 1988 issue.

My thanks also to Huntington Energy Systems (a JWP Company) and Richard Greco, for permission to use the art on page 98. To Ken Rabasca and Kim Mitchell of Greenstone & Rabasca Advertising, for providing material used in the comps and finished art chapters and for permission to reproduce the art on pages 64–71 and 85–89. To Scholastic Publications, for permission to reproduce the illustrations from *Maxx Trax II* (written by James Preller) on pages 91–97.

A special note of gratitude to Greg Glass, president of Design Tools and co-developer of Facet, for his patience, perseverance, and invaluable assistance. To Frank D'Aprile, for some timely hands-on instruction in the new (for me) area of three-dimensional design. To Robert Thornton, co-developer of Facet, for his never-failing encouragement and advice. To Sharon Larkin of Genigraphics Corporation, for technical assistance. To the Computer Graphics Lab at Old Westbury, New York, for technical assistance and imaging.

A special thanks also to Slidegrafix, Inc., for the QCR imaging of many of the slides used in this book—especially Michael Shuster, who not only supervised the imaging but who was also kind enough to read the manuscript with an eye to any possibly misleading statements on computer technology and who gave helpful advice on how to make the information understandable to artists.

Finally, my thanks to Glorya Hale and Julia Moore, editorial director and senior editor, respectively, at Watson-Guptill Publications, for their enthusiasm and help with the inception of this book. My gratitude also to Sue Heinemann, artist and senior editor at Watson-Guptill, who knew what I wanted to say—and to whom—and who stubbornly but patiently made sure I carried out that intention.

PICTURE CREDITS

It may be of interest to note that the two-dimensional computer graphics in this book were, for the most part, done on the Genigraphics PGP system. Most of the work is my own, but I gratefully acknowledge the contributions of Elaine Raphael (who did the artwork on pages 12, 62, and 140, and collaborated with me on the annual report covers on pages 73–81), Steve Rivera of Slidegrafix, Inc. (who did both business slides on page 101), and Joe Cychosz and Dave Plunkett (who did the three-dimensional art on page 132).

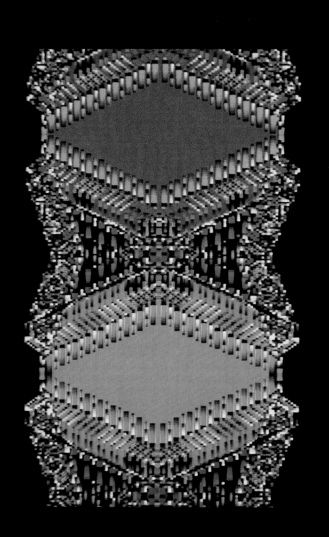

CONTENTS

INTRODUCTION

"Curiosity killed the cat." That cautionary cliché has passed through my mind several times in the last few years, once or twice even giving me pause. For it was curiosity that first tempted me to investigate computer graphics. Nothing in my training or professional background prepared me for something as foreign as a computer paint system. But it sounded intriguing, so I decided to see one firsthand.

We've all experienced moments in life that are memorable—not necessarily world-shaking, but unforgettable . . . such as the first taste of a wonderful food. These moments of discovery change one's life in ways both large and small. Such was the case with my first direct experience of computer art.

While touring the Computer Graphics Lab at the New York Institute of Technology in Old Westbury, New York—a research and development facility—I was invited to draw on a paint system. I picked up the stylus and drew a simple sketch of a horse. It was surprisingly easy and felt very natural—but it wasn't unforgettable. What happened next was that the demonstrator reached out to the keyboard and hit a couple of buttons; instantly my simple drawing became a brilliant, kaleidoscopic chain of moving colors. It was as if my horse had suddenly come alive.

I was thrilled—and hooked. Since that time, in professional workshops, at colleges, or with clients, I have seen my own initial reaction repeated in others, an experience akin to magic.

Now, six years later, wiser and more experienced, my enthusiasm is still intact, and I am more deeply involved than ever in this art form. Mastering this medium is, as with most complex techniques, an ongoing process, in which each new plateau reveals another height to be challenged. In some ways mastering the computer to create art resembles learning to ride a horse. At first one feels awe and fear in the presence of such power. Little by little, however, one gains control and confidence—always aware, of course, of the tremendous potential at the other end of the being. Eventually, the rider is confident enough to allow control to give way to collaboration, so that horse and rider become one. In like manner the artist learns to collaborate with the computer to produce an art that is an amalgam of creativity and technology.

What is needed is an adventurous, risk-taking approach to art—a curiosity about the new, much of which lies, unknown and unseen, around a dozen corners. Yes, *curiosity*—that word again. Of course, today we don't take those old sayings seriously. Anyhow, there's another old adage about cats, reassuring us that after all "a cat has nine lives." Well, so do artists.

PART ONE

THE NEW STUDIO

MEMO
11/19   7:45 A.M.

From: R. T. Stonewall, President
        One Stop Computers, Inc.
To: M. R. Jackson, Account Executive
        Smart Guys Advertising, Inc.
Re: New marketing approach for our
        latest, compact computer graphics
        workstation

Up to now our print and TV ads have empha-sized our product's versatility, ease of use, full-color output, and low cost. Fine, but do you know, Ms. Jackson, the most pressing prob-lem facing designers and illustrators today? Well, I'll tell you. It's their overhead, and it's spelled R-E-N-T. They can't expand because the good locations in big cities cost too much and traditional studios need too much room. The answer—move to Nowheresville? No. Buy a One Stop computer graphics worksta-tion. It's like renting a loft and hiring three artists all in one. Let's see some ideas. OK?

MEMO
11/19   11:45 A.M.

From: M. R. Jackson, Account Executive
        Smart Guys Advertising, Inc.
To: R. T. Stonewall, President
        One Stop Computers, Inc.

Good idea, R. T. Here's a rough storyboard (done on your One Stop paint system) to test one idea. Hope you like it.

Hey guys, another art studio. . . . Remember the big one last week, the one we moved across the river to that factory building next to the sewage disposal plant?

Yeh—what was it?—436 boxes, not counting those desks. And those huge files.

Well, here we are. You feel strong today?

Hello, Finicky Movers. Oh, excuse me, this must be the wrong . . .

Hi. Nope, this is it. Don't need this big rent anymore. We're moving to smaller offices in a nice old town-house in midtown. Here's the address.

(Logo tumbles through space to form one compact shape.)

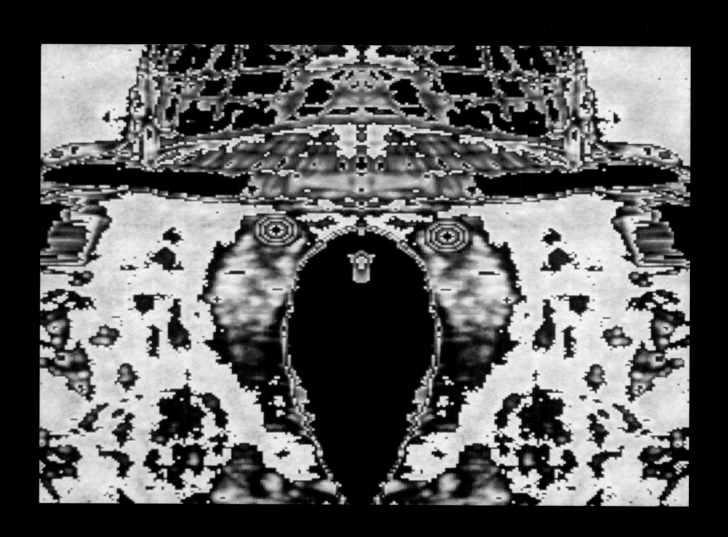

HARDWARE: THE COMPUTER GRAPHICS WORKSTATION

The move is over. It's time to unpack the boxes, set up the equipment, and take a close look at a typical computer graphics workstation. First, there are some familiar items—a desk and what appears to be a drawing board and a pen. But there is also a TV monitor—that's definitely unusual. And there's not a pad of paper in sight—that's strange. What we have is a combination of the old and the new, deliberately designed into computer paint systems so that traditionally trained artists can feel at home while they learn the new technology.

Actually, if you think about the traditional design process, you'll begin to understand how a computer graphics workstation operates. Most often, before the hands-on designing gets underway, there is an "analysis," or brainstorming, session between the client and designer. Then the challenge shifts to the designer, who must turn the ideas discussed into concrete visual images. In the first step, using anything from thumbnail sketches to full-color roughs, the designer experiments with as many options as possible. The next step is to identify and develop the most promising options. Finally, in the third stage, the designer brings two or three of the best designs to the degree of completion usually referred to as the "finished comp"—something the client can actually hold, examine, and take back to the office.

These three steps in the creation of a finished design—analysis, design realization, and finished comp—are mirrored in the computer graphics workstation by devices that input, process, and then output information. With this in mind, let's track a job as it goes through the computer.

This image combines the old with the new: an illustration done in traditional media, scanned into a computer, and reworked into something totally different.

THE BASIC DESIGN PROCESS

The designer begins by sketching the ideas that have emerged from analysis of the project. In place of a pad of visualizing paper and felt-tip markers, there is the monitor, the digitizer pad, and the stylus. The stylus, through a depressable point, makes contact with electronic sensors in the pad. These messages, or commands, are routed through the microprocessor, or central processing unit (CPU), and translated into an image on the monitor screen. The stylus and pad combo is an input, or locator, device. Because it responds to and reflects the actions of the artist's hand so immediately, it is also called an interactive device. The important point here is the similarity of sensation between working on a computer and traditional drawing.

After each sketch is completed it is put away, not in a drawer, but in the computer's storage device—a disk. Using the computer's keyboard, the designer names each sketch and stores it in the paint program's "picture file." From there it can easily be recalled to the monitor screen.

The initial sketches are just to get the idea down. But as the idea becomes more focused, the designer may feel a need to use some existing images: photos, artwork, or perhaps typographic elements. Traditionally, one might use stats, photocopies, lucies, or the like. At a computer graphics workstation the job is done with an input device, usually a video camera or scanner (this process is sometimes called "an image grab"). The device is capable of transforming pre-existing two-dimensional images and three-dimensional ob-

jects into digital information so that they can be "read" and stored by the computer. And once these images exist on the computer disk, they can be changed, enhanced, and recombined in ways that surpass traditional methods.

All of this sketching and scanning is processed through the central processing unit, which contains the electronic circuitry necessary to basic computing along with add-on electronic boards that provide color and connections to various input and output devices, among other things.

The central processing unit also houses the storage devices (disks), which contain the software programs, or computer graphics toolkit. Through the software, the designer can manipulate the image in new and exciting ways (see pages 21–59).

This brings us to the final step of the design process: the actual piece of work. Just as in a traditional design project, thumbnails may become full-size roughs, which are transformed into finished sketches, which then become finished comps. With a computer graphics workstation, examples from all of these stages can be viewed on the monitor.

"But," you may ask, "what does the designer hand the client?" True, a client can view the design on the monitor, but what can he or she take away?

Just as the computer graphics workstation can transform tangible material (photos, artwork) into digital form using input devices, it can now reverse the process and turn digital information into an actual picture on paper or film by using output devices.

This simplified diagram of a computer graphics workstation shows the basic flow of an idea through the system. The digitizer pad and electronic stylus allow the artist to draw directly. The images and commands are fed into the central processing unit (CPU), which sorts out the instructions and then displays the resulting picture on the monitor. Depending on the system, there may be both a full-color monitor (red-green-blue) and a black-and-white monitor (monochrome), or just a color monitor. The keyboard can be used to input text.

This diagram shows some more sophisticated input and output devices. In addition to drawing directly, the artist can scan in information through a color video camera or a black-and-white scanner. The image on the monitor can then be changed into hard copy through an output device such as a film recorder, printer, or videotape recorder, as discussed on the following pages.

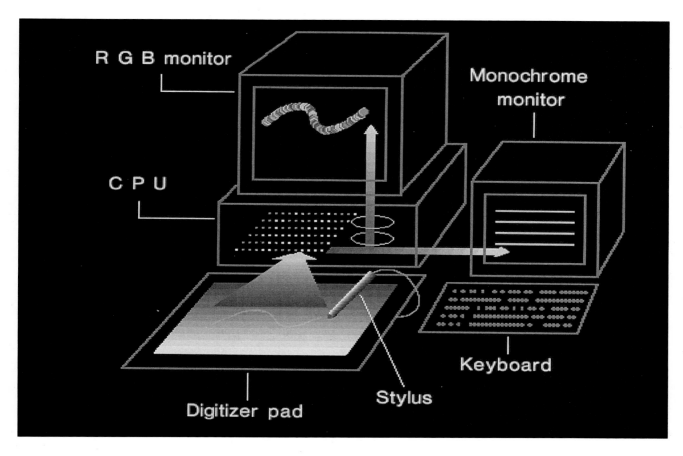

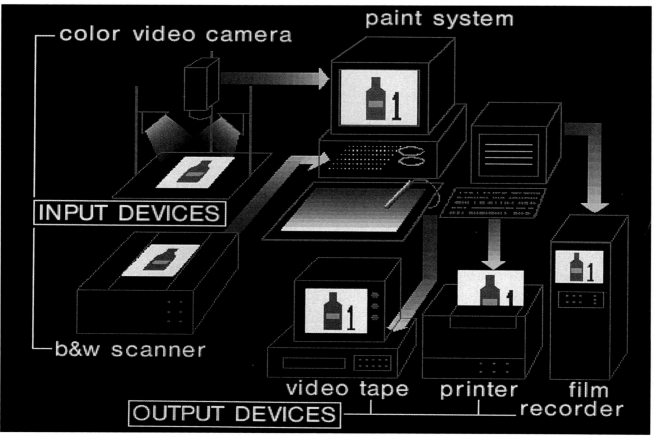

Suppose that, after seeing a new logo design on your monitor, the client wants to send copies of it to other company members before making a final decision. With the computer graphics workstation, you have several options.

One form of output—cited by some experts as one of the best currently available—is thermal transfer printing. This process produces a full-color image on paper that is roughly comparable to a finished marker comp. Color fidelity is good, although there are some problems in the translation of the light-based colors on the screen to the pigment-based colors on paper. Based on the reactions of those who have used them, thermal transfer prints do the job and then some.

But what if the client wants to present the new logo design to a wider audience? Here the computer graphics workstation offers two choices: slides or video.

To produce color slides of an image on the monitor, the quickest, most direct, and least expensive method is to set your camera up on a tripod, aim it at the screen, and take the picture. It's best to use daylight film, but if you want even quicker results you can use instant film.

For sharper, denser, and in some cases higher-resolution images, it is best to use a film recorder, which is hooked up directly to the computer graphics workstation. Without getting technical, suffice it to say that the path from the monitor image to the recorded slide can be bumpy. Each software package must have a specific "driver" for the specific film recorder you are using. And the high-resolution

digital recorders sometimes behave like high-strung thoroughbreds needing constant care and fine-tuning. Nevertheless, once the kinks are worked out, a digital film recorder is an invaluable tool.

Another handy device is a Polaroid printer, just in case the client wants a quick print of the slide. With this tool, you can make prints in several sizes, up to 8 × 10 inches.

Finally, you can equip the computer graphics workstation with a video module, allowing you to provide the client with a videotape of the design. In this case, you might decide to include some form of animation to increase the visual impact (see the discussion on pages 104–117).

Prints, slides, and video in hand, the client now goes away happy (for the moment). Think back through the process. The computer graphics workstation allows you to do many jobs "in house" that previously could only have been handled by outside services. It not only saves a great deal of time (and thus money), but, most important, it provides design flexibility.

Of course, success with computer graphics isn't as simple as buying the right hardware. There are two other important components. One, obviously, is the artist—the real creative force. The other is the paint or design software—the program that enables the imaginative designer to realize an idea and bring it to completion. Without good graphics software, the entire computer graphics workstation—the central processing unit, scanners, monitors, and printers—might just as well be left in the cartons.

With this thermal transfer print, the image on the screen is reproduced on paper. It gives the client something concrete to take away; moreover, it is relatively easy to print additional copies. Most printers offer two sizes: 8½ × 11 and 11 × 17 inches. But remember: your paint program must have special software, or drivers, to output images to a specific printer (see the cautionary tale on page 19).

Compare the color in this image, shot directly from the monitor, with the color in the thermal transfer print. To take this picture, I used a 35mm camera mounted on a tripod. The film was Ektachrome 64; the lens opening ranged from 1.8 to 4; the shutter speed from ¼ to ½ a second. In shooting directly from the screen, remember to keep the room dark and—most important—use a tripod, as the shutter speed is slow. Experiment with a roll of film first, trying different speeds and exposures. That way you'll know what works.

This image was taken with a digital recorder (a Matrix QCR D4/2). Digital recorders usually give more information than analog ones and are preferred for preparing slides for print reproduction.

This image is a color print, made by a Polaroid printer from a 35mm slide. A Polaroid printer is useful if you need to make a quick print from a slide for the client to take home. You can even do 8 × 10-inch prints on this machine.

A QUESTION OF COMPATIBILITY

Manufacturers of hardware constantly claim compatibility with the most popular computer company. What is not stated by manufacturers and retail salespeople is that hardware compatibility is not the whole story. A common example concerns peripherals such as printers.

A graphic designer already knowledgeable about computers decided to buy a dot-matrix printer. He was advised by a technical consultant to buy Brand A's Model X. Brand A was very popular and its printers were widely used. Model X was a new, improved dot-matrix printer but not a new technology. The designer expected to use it with paint software that was also widely used. All the parts were advertised as compatible. When the designer hooked up his printer to the computer, it worked fine . . . until he tried printing something from the paint software. He then discovered that although the paint program supported other models from Brand A, it did not support Model X. A phone call to the paint software developers proved discouraging, as they had no plans to write a support program for that particular model.

What went wrong? Both the designer and the technical consultant made assumptions based on the overall compatibility and popularity of the two products. The moral: Assume nothing. If you already own software, buy peripherals that it definitely supports. Don't believe a salesperson or software developer who claims that in the near future x, y, or z printers will be supported. Plans and models change; so do schedules. If you have hardware that you really want to use, buy only software that supports that specific piece of hardware.

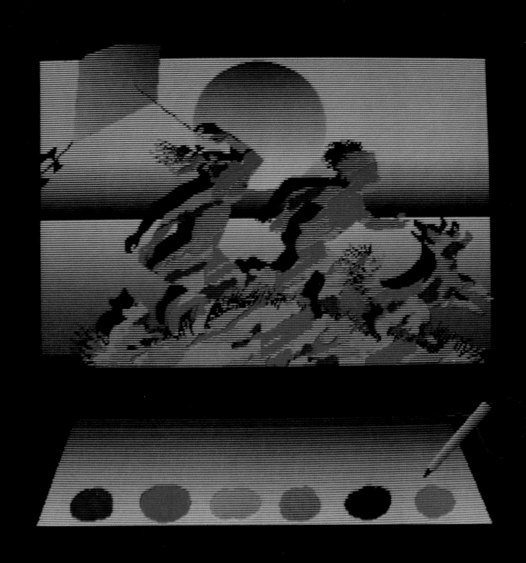

SOFTWARE: THE COMPUTER GRAPHICS TOOLKIT

Look around a traditional design studio. There are brushes and pens in varied sizes, markers and pencils in a rainbow of colors, T-squares and triangles, point and pica measures, knives and blades, pieces of acetate and tracing paper—the list could go on forever. One thing is certain: illustrators and designers need lots of tools and materials.

Computer graphics doesn't change the need for a variety of tools; it just changes the form. Instead of purchasing many different pieces of equipment, you buy a graphics software package, which encompasses the different capabilities you need. Essentially the software is a set of instructions that allows you to "talk" to your computer and tell it what you want done. You might ask it to draw a line of a certain width in a certain color from point A to point B, or you might specify different-size rectangles and circles.

To get an idea of the possibilities, take a look at the menus on the following pages. Although different graphics software packages will offer slightly different menus, the basic functions will be similar. The point is not so much *how* this particular program works, but *what* the computer can do. You'll be surprised at how well the computer can carry out mundane design chores and how it can actually encourage you to be creative.

This cover proposal for a children's book on computer painting is meant to convey the wonder and excitement of the new computer graphics toolkit.

A MENU OF CHOICES

Sitting at a computer graphics workstation is a bit like sitting at a restaurant. The first thing you're presented with is a menu—in this case, a listing of the various functions available to you on your particular paint program. To whet your appetite, here are some of the choices usually available:

- *Color.* In all probability you will have literally millions of colors to choose from in setting up a palette for a particular project. Indeed, there are probably more colors available than you can even imagine. There's no way you could get all these subtle hues by mixing traditional media. Plus you don't have to worry about running out of a color in the middle of a job—it's always there.
- *Brushes.* By selecting different "brushes" you can vary the weight, the shape, and even the texture of your marks. You can also create your own brushes, designing a simple symbol like a bird that you can then "paint" with. In this way the computer allows you to custom-design your own artistic tools—at no extra cost.
- *Automatic drawing.* To get rid of some of the drudgery of design, you can simply instruct the computer to draw circles or boxes of a certain size. That frees your energy so you can focus on more creative tasks.
- *Fill function.* With this handy function, you can fill in outlined shapes automatically, without working laboriously, stroke after stroke. And the computer is neat: it stays within the outline (as long as there are no gaps).

- *Copying tools.* If you want to draw a symmetrical image, you can simply draw one half and then mirror or "flop" it to create the other half. And there are other, similar "services" available on a computer that eliminate the need to send things outside, to a stat house. You can, for example, scale, rotate, copy, mirror, enlarge, or reduce any image in the pictures files.
- *Photographic possibilities.* In addition to the copying functions just mentioned, some software allows you to solarize or posterize photos that have been scanned in. You can shrink the photos in one dimension while stretching them in another. You can also retouch images and silhouette them. If the image you've scanned in is black and white, you can colorize it (much as they're doing now with old movies); or you can make a color image black and white.
- *Save function.* It's important to remember that any image you create on the monitor is ephemeral—unless and until you save it. Not only does saving an image allow you to recall it whenever you want, but it enables you to experiment more freely, changing the image in part or in its entirety, without losing the original. You can thus easily show a client the original with several variations (each saved separately, under different names). This capability is one of computer painting's greatest virtues. It certainly goes a long way toward eliminating Excedrin Headache #1 for both artist and client.

This is an example of an icon type of menu. Each symbol represents a function. In this case the airbrush, or spray can, function has been selected. The rectangle in the upper left of the large rectangle shows the various densities of spray. (Software: Dr. Halo III from Media Cybernetics)

This photograph shows a pull-down menu for a three-dimensional program. The items in the central rectangle can be selected by simply pointing at them with a cursor. (Software: Facet 3D design program CGL)

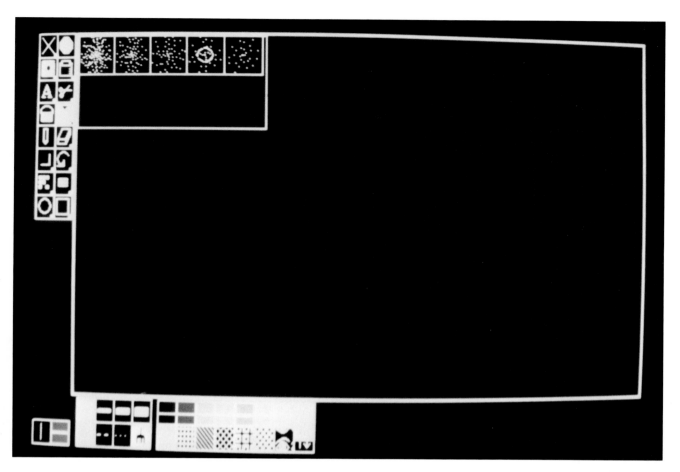

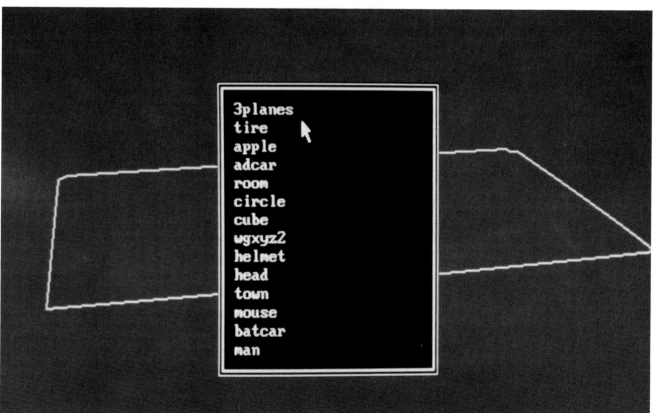

DETERMINING COLOR

How many jars and flat files would be needed to store 16.7 million shades of watercolor and colored paper? That is the potential range of a typical computer paint system. Admittedly, 16.7 million is probably a bit more than most artists need, and many systems permit only 256 colors to be displayed on the screen at any one time. The important point is not the final number but the availability of such variety and flexibility. Mixing and matching colors becomes an exciting adventure. What is really unprecedented is that now you can completely change the color scheme of a picture *after* it has been painted, and you can do it quickly, without risk of losing the original.

How does this magic take place? In electronic, light-based color red, green, and blue are the primary colors. This is in contrast to traditional paint or pigment color, where the primaries are red, yellow, and blue. In computer painting, then, all the other colors—yellows, browns, oranges, purples, grays—are combinations of at least two of the red-green-blue trio. Another point to remember is that in computer painting, total saturation of all colors produces white, whereas in traditional painting mixing all the colors together creates a dark mud.

But how is computer color manipulated? Most computer paint systems allow for change in the three basic characteristics of color:

hue, or actual color; *saturation*, the degree of grayness; and *luminosity*, a color's light-dark value. You can adjust a color in all three categories at once or one at a time.

Consider, for example, a picture with a bright blue sky. Perhaps you feel that the bright blue should be changed but are not quite sure of the direction: should the color remain blue but become a bit grayer? Or is the blue simply too light? Or, finally, should the blue be replaced completely with another color? Each of these changes can be investigated fully. How many changes can you go through in making a decision? Well, as was just indicated, many paint systems allow for color variations of up to 16.7 million.

A QUESTION OF NUMBERS

Though I try to avoid the subject, there are times when the mathematics involved in computers must be addressed—even if only in the simplest form. A perfect example comes up in a discussion of computer color: Just how many different colors are available to the artist? Most paint systems advertise 16.7 million colors. But that number refers to the potential variety, not necessarily how many colors the artist will be able to use on any one picture. Most of the color work in this book, for example, was done on a system with 16.7 million potential colors, but only 256 were available at one time. From a practical point of view, this restriction rules out certain artistic procedures, such as scanning in and then retouching a full-color photograph. For that procedure, you need the full 16.7 million.

Obviously, an artist interested in full-color capabilities needs to look beyond the general claim of 16.7 million colors and ask about the number of colors available on the screen. A

quick way to find out is to look at the specifications of the graphics card. Computers that have an 8-bit card display only 256 colors at one time. To display all 16.7 million colors on the screen at once, you need a 24- or 32-bit card.

What are the advantages of this greater color density, besides the retouching ability just mentioned? An important plus is that the "jaggie" look is greatly reduced. This is due, not to higher resolution, but to a greater color range, producing much more subtle transitions between one area of color and the next. These subtleties are important for three-dimensional modeling and rendering programs (see Part Three). Print applications also need 24-bit graphics to approximate traditional airbrush effects.

Are there any advantages to the 8-bit cards, with 256 colors? Surprisingly, yes. With an 8-bit system, you can do color cycling, which can be used for limited animation effects (see the discussion on page 110).

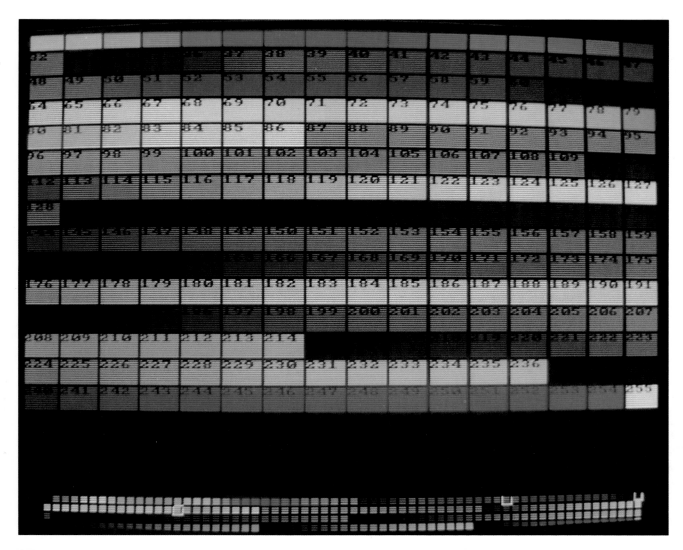

At the bottom of the screen you can see the normal palette for a system that can display 256 colors. The large palette in the center does not normally appear; it is shown here only to help clarify the selection process. Note that any of the colors here can be altered (there are over 16 million choices, even though only 256 are available at once). To do this, you can add or subtract color, electronically mixing color. But keep in mind that on the computer you're working with light-based color, not pigment.

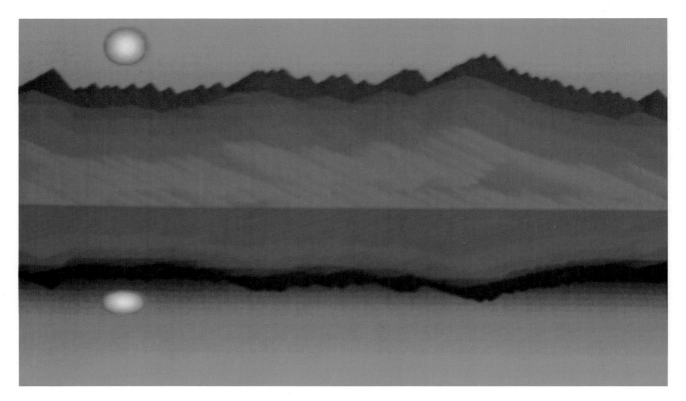

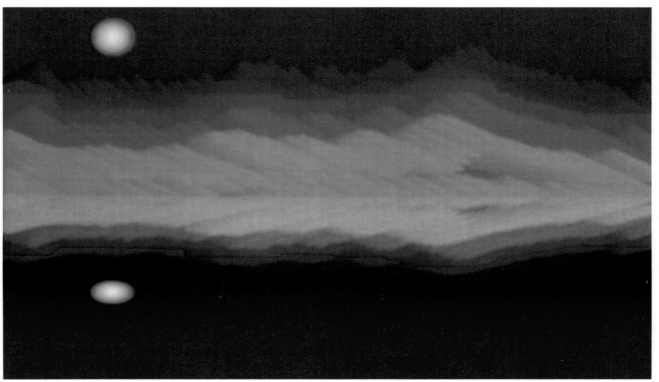

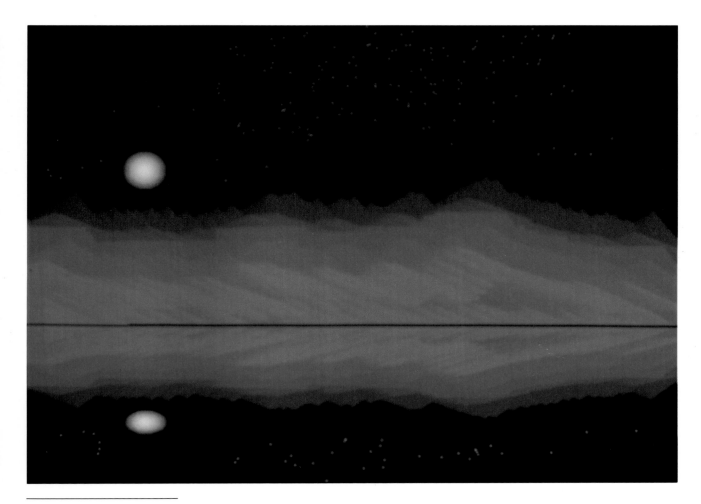

The variations in this landscape were easy to do on a computer. To create the initial scene, I made the mountains and then used the copying function to suggest a mirror reflection, at the same time changing the proportions to avoid an exact symmetry. Next I experimented with different color combinations just for fun. The ability to play with color in this way—without "ruining" your original design—is an invaluable boost to creativity. In the last version, note how I changed the composition and added some stars to create a deeper sense of space. But if I didn't like this, I could always go back to the initial version (provided I had saved it).

SELECTING A BRUSH

When you sit down to paint with traditional media, you must choose not only a color but also a brush (or other painting tool). On a computer the process is similar. Most paint systems offer an array of brushes in different sizes, from small (one or two pixels in width) to large, round dots. With these brushes, you can produce a single-weight line in any direction. There are also different linear brushes—vertical, horizontal, or oblique—which vary in weight and length.

Another kind of brush is the textured brush, made up of clusters of pixels. With this brush, you can simulate a variety of illustrative effects, from the painterly lines of drybrush to the precision of airbrush. As we will see later, this brush—or any of the other brushes just described—can be edited into a specific shape.

One thing you'll notice on the computer is that the brushstrokes have well-defined edges. There are, however, systems with brushes that allow you to produce a relatively soft-edged line—an effect referred to as "anti-aliasing." Essentially what happens is that the color in the brushstroke is automatically blended into the background color. The result is a reduction in the jagged, staircase look so often seen on medium-resolution computer systems. Some systems are completely anti-aliased, while others have special functions to accomplish this effect. Words like "filter," "blend," and "solid averaging" may be used to describe the blurring of edges between one color and another. In any case, anti-aliasing is very useful in imitating traditional airbrush effects.

Here is a sampling of brushes you can choose from. The arrows point to the individual brush shapes, while to the right you can see strokes characteristic of each brush. Notice how the stroke varies, depending on whether you move the mark vertically, horizontally, or diagonally, In this way the brush behaves like a calligraphy pen.

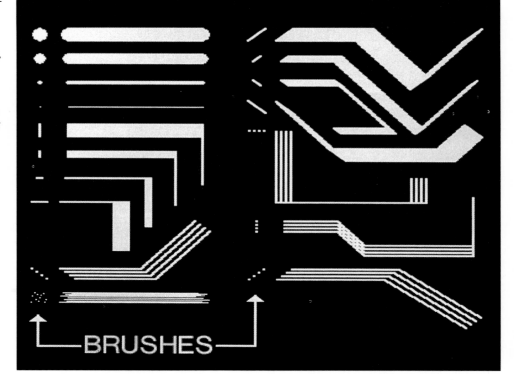

This scene was created with a textured brush, made up of many pixels. If you look closely, you can even see some of the pixels. The final image has a pastel-like quality, and, indeed, the process of making it was similar to pastel painting. The brush was scumbled over areas, and the whole was built up gradually, in layers.

Although both drawings here evidence jagged edges, or jaggies, the lines on the right show the effect of anti-aliasing. In the blowup you can see more clearly how the value is modulated, or averaged to the surface color, to "blur" the edges.

Having selected a color and brush, you're ready to begin in earnest on your computer. A good way to get comfortable with the equipment is to do some freehand sketching. It's not that different from sitting at a desk and drawing with a pen. True, it may be momentarily disconcerting to draw on one surface (the digitizer pad) while looking at another (the monitor). But usually this sensation is short-lived and never noticed again. Anyhow, the stylus should feel familiar (if you're using a mouse, it may take a little more practice to feel as comfortable with it).

Keep in mind that the stylus is your fundamental link to the computer. By pressing down slightly with the tip, you can select a location on the screen or pick an item from the menu. You can also draw freehand with the stylus, depressing the tip for the duration of the stroke. (The mouse operates in much the same way—it's primarily the feel that's different.)

Now what about the quality of line on a computer? For many artists, especially illustrators, line quality (in pencil or pen) is synonymous with style. One look at a drawing by Hirschfeld is sufficient to identify its creator. A drawn line is like a signature—delicate or bold, rhythmic or scratchy. Drawing on the computer is not intended to compete with what can be accomplished in traditional media. But that doesn't mean that an artist can't draw freely on a computer; even calligraphy can be done. As the technology improves, it becomes more and more possible to achieve a hand-drawn look, if that is what you want. Some systems provide pressure-sensitive equipment that allows you to vary the width of a single stroke. But, in any case, you will have a variety of brushes, enabling you to produce thin, thick, oblique, or textured lines.

These letters were drawn with oblique brushes, in three different sizes. Two advantages of using the computer for calligraphy are that you can easily "erase" any mistakes and that the brush never deviates from its angle. On the other hand, the "jaggies" do interfere with the flow of the letterforms to some extent.

These two sketches for the knight's horse shown on page 57 were done on the computer, using the freehand drawing mode. Although the line has a different quality from a pencil or a brush line, you can obviously draw quite freely, in your own style. Moreover, you can take a line sketch and quickly add some tone, without destroying the original line sketch in your picture file.

LETTING THE COMPUTER DO THE WORK

Tradition has it that a young artist entering the field has to apprentice by doing the noncreative, menial work that is ever-present in a studio: pasteups, mechanicals, mounting, mat cutting—the artist's version of "boot camp." Most artists who have gone through it have hated it. But with the arrival of computer paint systems, that kind of apprenticeship may be a thing of the past.

Straight lines, neat rectangles, perfect circles, smooth curves, mat borders, outlined boxes; in short, every studio activity that requires sharp razor blades, nonsplattering ruling pens, steady hands, clean fingers, and technical facility—all those demanding but uncreative jobs can now be done by the computer. All you have to do is select the appropriate function from the menu—straight lines or boxes, for example—and then "tell" the computer how long a line or how big a box you want. The computer does the rest, drawing the line or box between the points you have indicated. In this way, by taking care of the tedious tasks, the computer frees you to concentrate on the truly creative aspects of the project.

Tracing and outlining are also a snap on the computer. Moreover, outlined areas—which in the traditional studio would have to be filled in with either paint or colored paper—can be filled in by the computer in less time than it takes to describe it.

The "fill" function is one of those tools that really set computer painting apart as a totally new medium. Once the outline is drawn, you can select this function and automatically fill the enclosed area with a selected color. As long as the area is completely surrounded by either a line or the edge of another color, the "fill" color will stay within the designated area. (But if there is even a tiny [one pixel] gap in the perimeter, the fill will spill out into other areas.) It is not hard to imagine how valuable such a function is. Beyond the time saved in applying color, there is the bonus of design flexibility. If an area can so easily be filled and refilled with a color, the artist is no longer restricted by the time and labor considerations associated with the traditional methods of changing a color. A whole picture can be recolored in a few minutes, as long as the color areas are discrete.

These straight lines were all drawn by the computer. All I did was to select the line mode from the menu, choose a color and a brush, and then indicate with my stylus where I wanted the beginning and the end of the line.

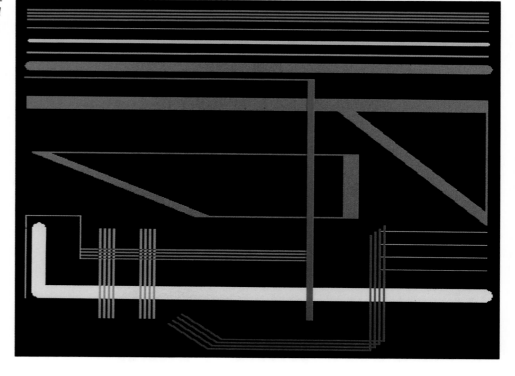

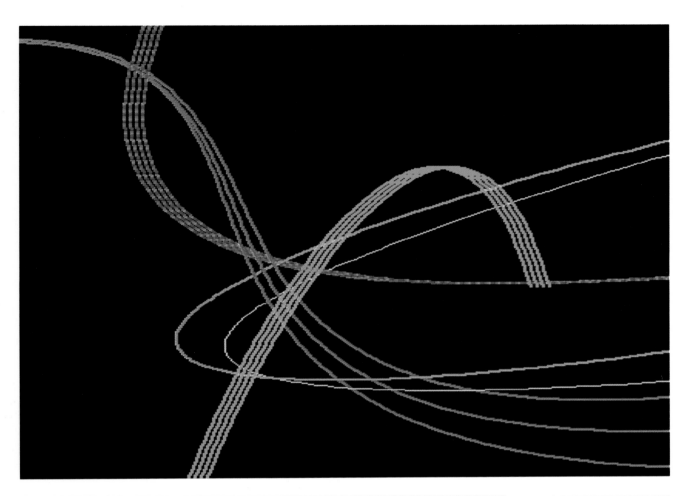

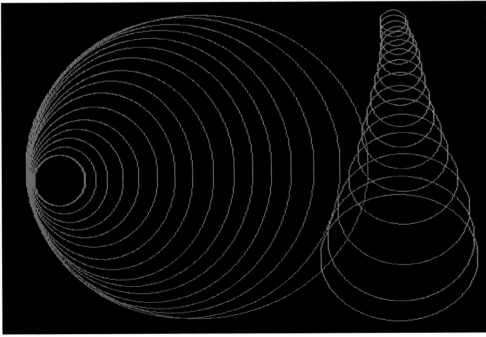

The curves were drawn au-
tomatically, using an
oblique brush. What hap-
pens is that you first "pre-
view" the curve, manipulat-
ing it until you get the curve
you want. Then the com-
puter redraws it in the exact
color or brush you want.

The circles were drawn in
much the same way as the
curves. Although the circles
themselves were drawn au-
tomatically, each was scaled
individually by eye in a pre-
view fashion.

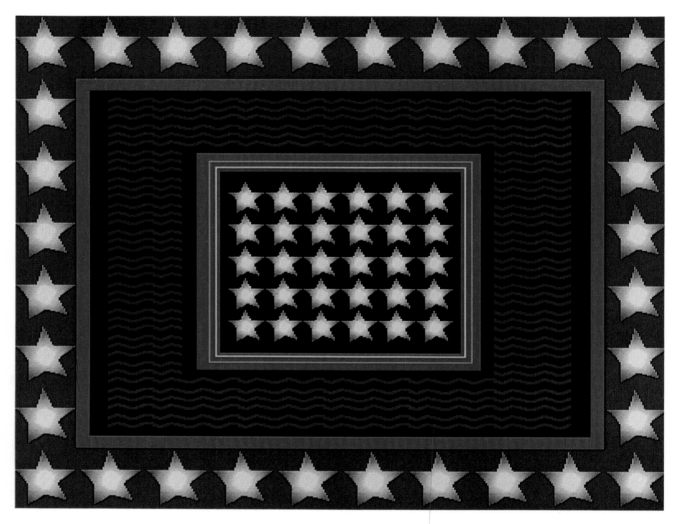

Above

By selecting the trim, or border, function, you can automatically create a mat in the color or pattern of your choosing. The star pattern in the image here was created with a picture brush (see pages 38–39).

Right

Drawing with rectangles is similar to drawing with straight lines. After selecting the box mode, you simply move the cursor to control the size of the rectangle. You can overlap the rectangles, abut them, or keep them separate. And, of course, you can easily change the color scheme.

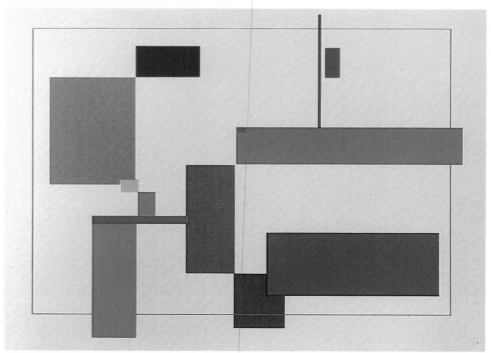

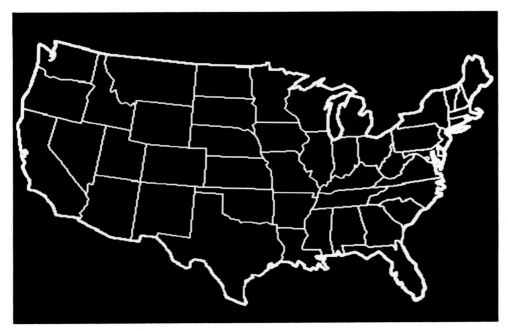

Here the original map was traced onto the screen using a small dot brush. After selecting the fill function from the menu and a color from my palette, all I did was touch the area to be filled in and watch as the computer filled it with the selected color. Remember that the area to be filled has to be completely outlined first to keep the color from spilling out. After all the areas have been filled in, you can remove the outlines.

As just demonstrated, straight lines and clean edges are a breeze on the computer. But what about spacing and placement, two essential elements of layout and mechanical work? The computer tools that provide these capabilities are the grid and alignment functions. The grid function divides the screen into equal parts, with the size of the units determined by the artist. If the alignment mode is on, lines, brushmarks, and shapes can be placed only on the grid's intersections, guaranteeing equal spacing and accurate placement. These two tools are perfect for studio work such as graphs, type and letter spacing, and pasteups, but they can also help in the creation of fabric designs or anything else employing a repeating pattern.

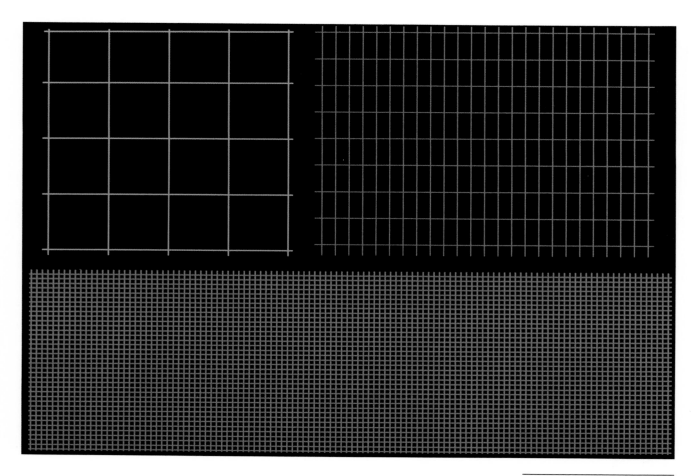

These are just a few of the different-size grids you can easily create. Although the primary purpose of the grid is practical, it obviously also provides opportunities for design experimentation.

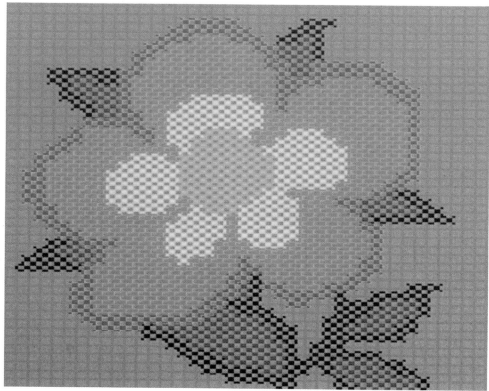

As you can see, the alignment mode is something eighteenth-century needlepoint artists would have loved. To get the effect shown here, I first edited a brush to resemble a characteristic needlepoint stitch. Then each such brushstroke was placed, using the align mode, on a tight grid. You can see this clearly in the detail.

DESIGNING WITH A PICTURE BRUSH

Another useful tool for creating repeating patterns or fabric designs is the picture brush—also referred to as a pattern brush. The best comparison is to a rubber stamp, with which you can reproduce an image many times, stamping it here and there, wherever you want, across a piece of paper. With a computer-generated rubber stamp, or picture brush, you can do the same thing but in a more precise and multicolored fashion.

The exact manner of creating a picture brush varies from system to system. Essentially, however, what you do is to isolate and then save a particular area—in any shape you want—of the color screen. The size of the saved area cannot exceed certain limits, imposed by the program—but these limits are usually dictated by common sense. After all, if you're working on a 13 × 13-inch screen, you don't need a 6 × 6-inch brush. You can, however, create a very long, thin brush, as is shown on page 40.

Picture brushes come in many shapes and forms. You can design star picture brushes, hearts, flowers, tree symbols, or even miniature figures. The only limit really is your imagination, although it's probably best to start out with simple forms.

The uses of a picture brush also defy categorization. Remember that it is, by definition, a custom-designed brush. The artist alone determines how it will be used. There are, however, a few basic ways to use a picture brush. Most obviously, the rubber-stamping method is a quick, simple way of replicating something, be it a logo, multicolored texture, or symbol. By rubber stamping this form, you then create a larger pattern, as in a fabric or wallpaper design.

Rubber stamping can be done freehand or, for more exact results, with a grid in the alignment mode. This use, though effective for some designs, does not suggest painting in the traditional sense. But that, too, is possible with picture brushes. You can make gestural strokes or continuous lines, working either freehand or in the automatic line-making mode. In this case the character of the picture brush undergoes a radical change. The single image of the rubber stamp becomes blurred, and the effect may be unpredictable. That unpredictability is what intrigues. This is indeed a *new* painting tool.

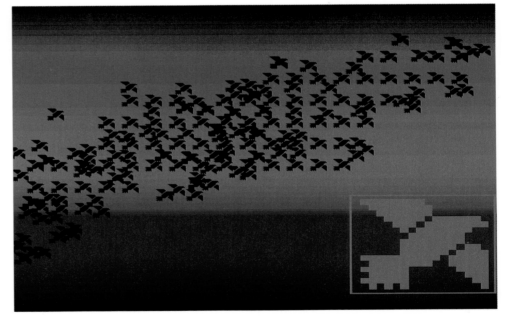

For this design I used a "bird" brush (shown in the blowup on the right), which I edited from a standard brush. I then "stamped" it in various places to create an overall pattern. Actually, there was a grid underneath this design. At first I worked with the grid, using the alignment mode, but then I turned it off and just stamped at will. As a result the completed image has a feeling of both order and randomness.

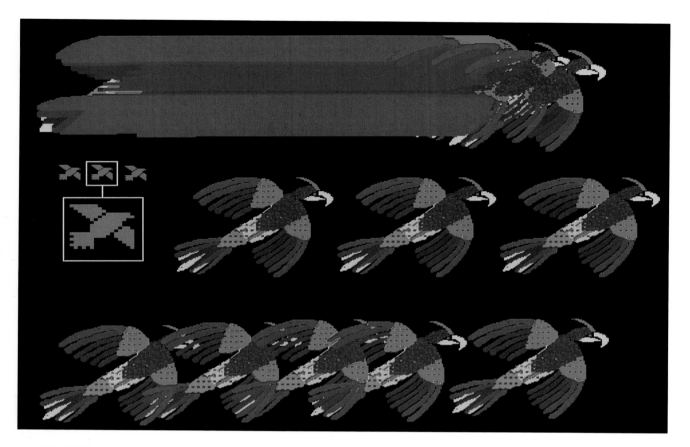

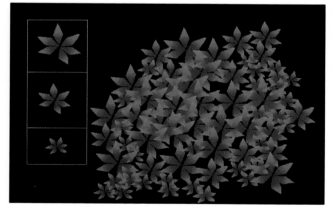

Left

For this design, I used three different-size "leaf" picture brushes (shown on the left). I placed them in different ways, letting them overlap to give a sense of space. On the computer it is easy to rework and rearrange this design. You can also go back in and alter some of the individual leaves, if you want a less patterned look.

Above

The parrot here is a picture (or pattern) brush, in contrast to the blue bird, which is an edited standard brush. One of the main differences is that an edited brush uses only one color at a time, while a picture brush is multicolored. Now take a look at the top row, which shows what happens when the picture brush is spread horizontally using the line function. The middle row shows a stamping effect, using the align mode to get even spacing. In the bottom row you can see one possibility of painting freehand with this kind of brush.

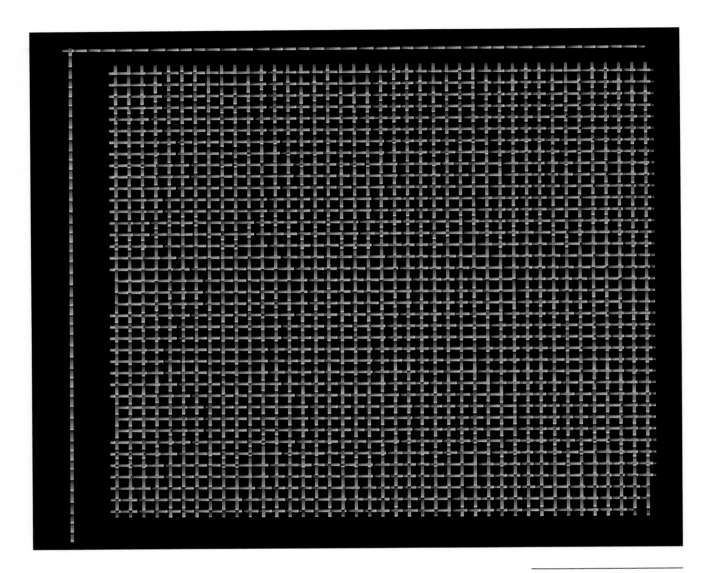

This textile-like woven pattern was created by crosshatching two picture brushes, using the alignment mode on a grid. The single lines at the top and on the left are the picture brushes. As you can see, the brushes themselves are like long, multicolored threads.

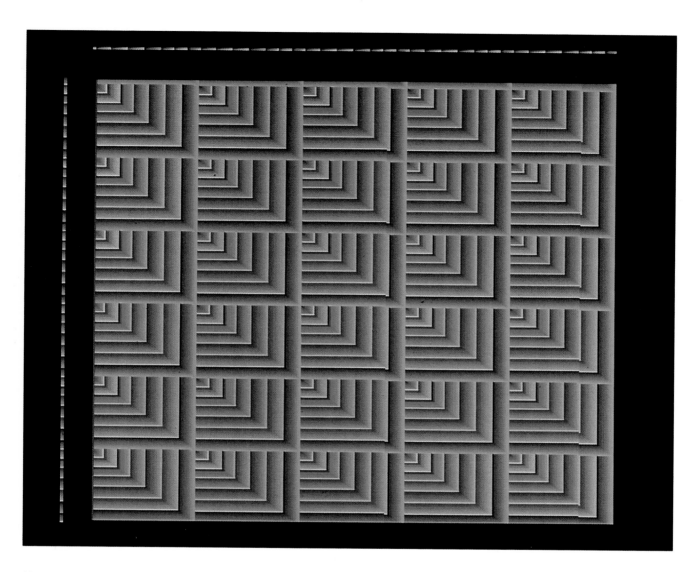

Above

Here the same two picture brushes have been painted over each other without using the grid and alignment, in a continuous stroke—creating a very different pattern. Again, the picture brushes are shown on the side to help you visualize their interaction.

Right

This image—surprisingly—is made with the same basic picture brushes as the previous example. What is different is the color palette. This is an important point to remember: changing the color palette can give the same configuration an entirely different look.

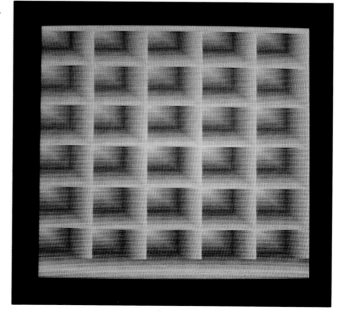

CREATING PAINTERLY EFFECTS

Although the application of the computer to mechanical design tasks is clear-cut, many artists wonder about its capabilities for more painterly illustrations. One way to think about this question is to ask: What do artists need to paint? Certainly color, brushes, and a surface. And, as we've seen, the computer provides all these. But there's more.

One time-honored painting tool is the palette knife, which can be used to spread pigment from one area of a canvas to another. The computer, of course, cannot provide the tactile pleasures associated with the palette knife technique. Some software packages, however, offer a "push" function, with which you can achieve very similar-looking results. Using this function, you can move solid colors or multicolored areas, spreading and smearing the colors and textures, much as you might with a palette knife.

Another traditional painting concern involves the interplay between transparency and opacity. Tempera and gouache are considered opaque media, while watercolor and inks are transparent. Oils and acrylics have the potential for both. In computer painting opacity is the norm: one color will usually completely cover another. It is, however, possible to get transparent effects, mimicking watercolor or oil glazes.

The function here is called "averaging." It resembles traditional tonal painting, in that it uses subtle shades of color as buffers between two contrasting values, creating a soft transition from light to dark. The difference is that you don't have to do the modeling—the computer does it for you, as in the detail of Leonardo's head on the facing page.

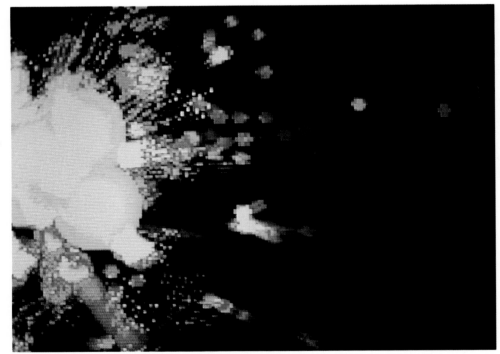

Here the push function has been used to create an explosive effect, with the colors almost shooting out from the star-like form. With the push function, you can spread the colors while working in either the freehand or in any one of the automatic line modes. Note that the push function is also an excellent tool for retouching because it uses colors that are in the image, eliminating the need to go back and forth to the color palette. Essentially, you correct a mistake by pulling a bit of the nearby color over the error.

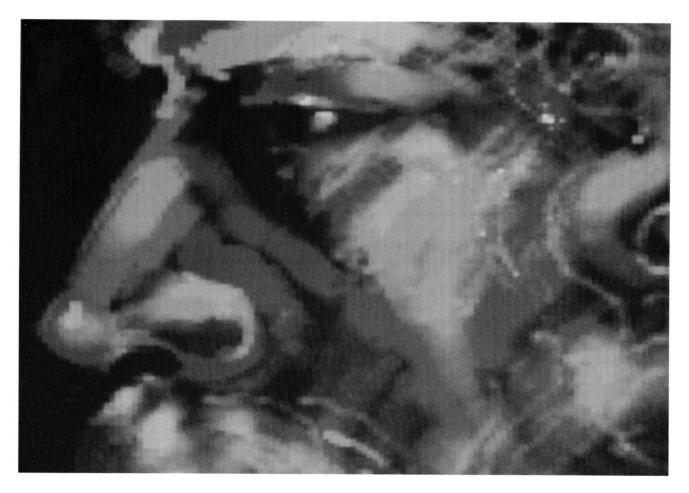

In this detail you can see the subtle tonal gradations possible with the averaging function. Basically, what happens is that the color is averaged over an area. You start with the darker tone (as shown in the small diagram), and then gradually, as you work over and over the area, it gets lighter. The computer essentially does the shading for you; you just tell it which color range to use.

But the averaging capability provides more than a way of imitating traditional soft-edged painting techniques. With some systems, you can use the averaging mode to produce a ghost, or transparent, images of the original picture brush. And this is where picture averaging resembles the transparency of glazing in painting, or superimposed impressions in printmaking, or multiple exposures in photography. Essentially, what you have here is a repeated image with many levels of intensity.

Yet another effect comes about through moving the image while it is in the picture-averaging mode. The result can be almost magical, with the image seemingly taking on a life of its own. What happens is that the different colors on the palette quite literally run or cycle through the image.

Actually, any image can be color-cycled if you're using an 8-bit system, with 256 colors on the screen. An entire color palette or only a part of it can be cycled through all or part of a picture. The speed of the cycling can be controlled, giving the designer an opportunity to view the image in various color combinations. Instead of painting yourself, you watch the computer paint the different possibilities, in a moving cycle, before you.

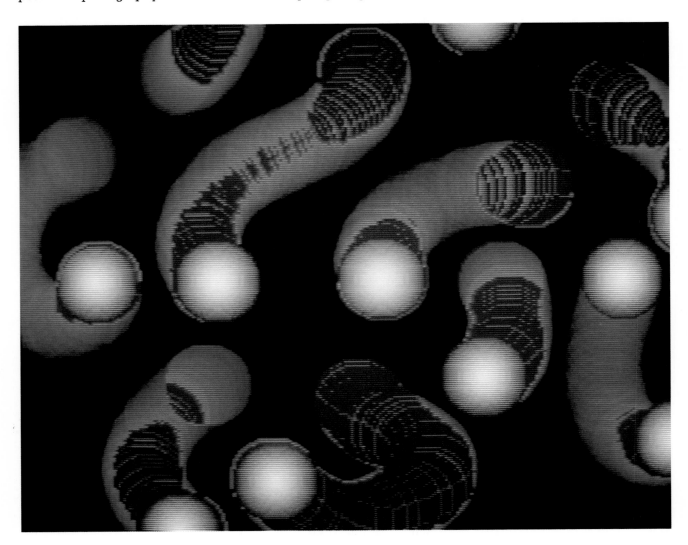

The letterforms show the effect of color cycling. But it's a dynamic process, so you'll have to use your imagination to "see" the colors on the palette cycling through the letters. If you look closely, you can see the separate bands of color, which change progressively, in accord with the palette. You can stop the process at any point, when you see the effect you want.

The transparent images were created by moving a ball-like picture brush while in the picture-averaging mode. More or less of the image appears, in a darker or brighter color, depending on how much time was spent in a particular spot. The results are not entirely predictable—you have to experiment with this technique for a while to get the feel of it.

PAINTING WITHOUT A BRUSH

So far we've looked at the computer's paint tools from a brush-oriented view of painting. But there are also brushless modes of painting available on the computer. These are new techniques, which compel traditionally trained artists to rethink their working methods.

Consider, for example, how you might paint a panel of horizontal colors on a computer. Thinking in traditional painting terms, you might choose a suitably sized brush, select an appropriate color palette, go into the alignment mode, and then paint the panel, "stroke" by "stroke."

But there's another, easier way to accomplish this task. Many paint systems can automatically create multicolored three or four-sided figures, ranging in size from small triangles to panels that fill the entire screen. To return to our example. Using this technique, the artist would first designate the panel's exact shape and location and then assign a color to each of the panel's four points. After that, the computer would do the rest, gradating or coloring the panel in accord with the color palette.

This rectangle was automatically shaded by the computer. All I did was to indicate that I wanted the darkest red in the top two corner points and the lightest red in the bottom two corners. The computer then filled in the rectangle, painting the range in between.

Here the darkest red was indicated for the two corner points on the left and the lightest red for the two corner points on the right.

In this example the dark red was selected for the top left and the lightest red for the other three points. Note how the color bends around, flowing outward from the top left toward these other points.

Here the opposite corners were selected for dark red or light red. Again, the color bends as it fills in the figure. By understanding your palette, you can create intriguing curved forms with this shading function.

This type of outline is what is often called a "rubber-band figure," in computer parlance. The name comes from its flexibility: it can be moved entirely; one or more of its points can be repositioned; it can be scaled up or down; and it can be rotated. When its position and shape are set, it can be colored by placing a tone at each of its four points—using the same procedure as with the rectangle on pages 46–47.

Although the same process was used below as in the earlier example, the effect is strikingly different, due to the use of a multicolored palette. Both the palette arrangement and the selection of colors for the corner points determine the width and direction of the color bands.

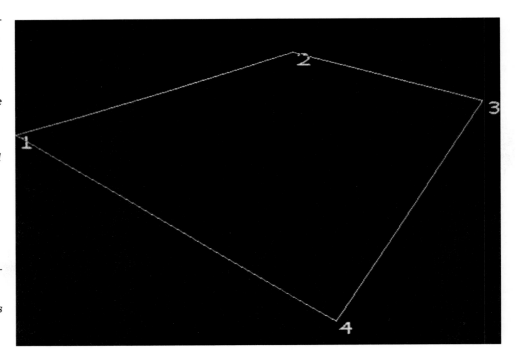

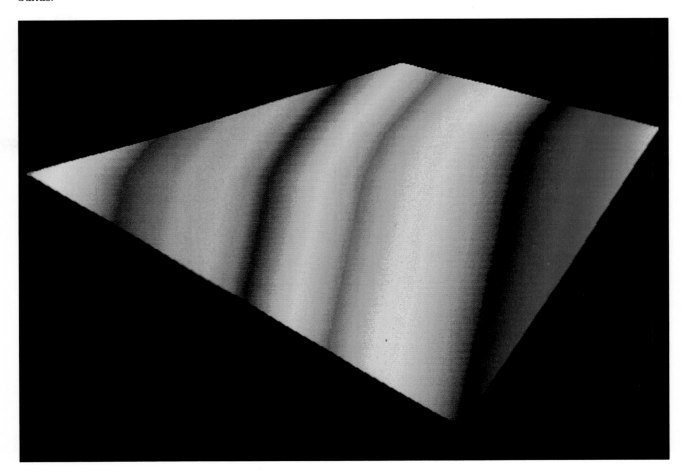

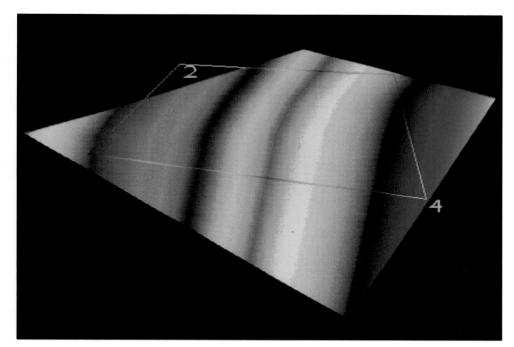

The same rubberband figure can easily be reduced and rotated and then placed over the original.

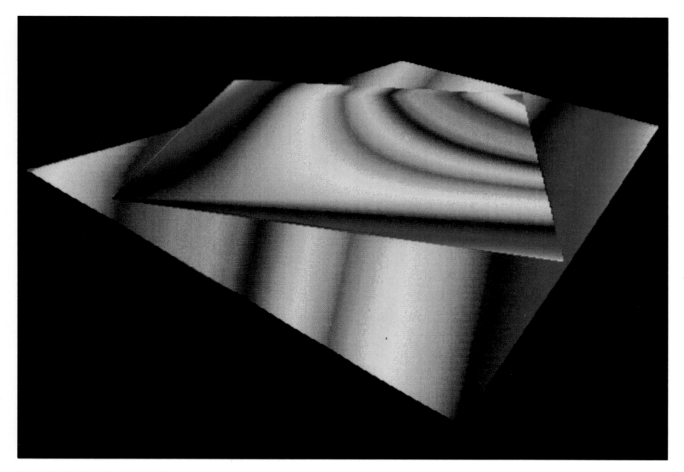

An entirely different effect is created by placing different colors at the corner points.

DEVELOPING THE HEAD OF AN ANDROID

The shading function has obvious potential for backgrounds and abstract designs, but can it be controlled enough to become a useful illustrative technique? The demonstration shown here should answer that question. The subject—a robot-like head—is well suited to the angular but smoothly shaded planes that are the hallmark of this unique computer painting technique.

The first step with a task like this is the same as with any traditional illustration job: to do some quick sketches and check out different reference material. In this case I went through my own sketchbooks, which were full of pencil and pen-and-ink drawings of heads. The point is that computer graphics fits into the traditional creative process. It's simply an-

other medium, with its own characteristics and limitations.

Imagine that you'd chosen wood engraving as the medium for an illustration of an android. The basic artistic challenge would be the same: how to translate your vision into a stylistically defined image. To do this, you'd need proficiency in your chosen medium, as well as design and drawing skills. Computer graphics is no different.

But what about the specific process? Here, working from my pencil sketches, I did several linear drawings on the computer to define the planes of the head before arriving at the final outline. Then I designed my color palette, choosing about forty shades of blue to get a monochromatic effect. The rest was easy—I just placed the four-sided figure over each out-

lined plane and chose the appropriate color for each corner.

Admittedly, that's an oversimplification. To achieve a more compelling three-dimensional illusion, I reworked various areas and redesigned the color palette. Making constant revisions is typical of how most artists work—the major difference in this case being the ease and speed with which the computer makes the changes.

And the ease of making changes encourages experimentation. What would the head look like with different hues or darker values? What if dark and light were reversed? Would a different background add interest? What about altering the shape itself? Part of the excitement of the computer is that it allows you to indulge your artistic curiosity.

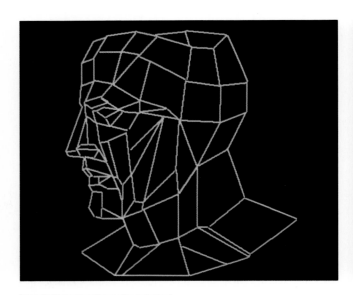

The first step on the computer is to outline the main planes of the head. To do this, I work from previous drawings (mostly in pencil). I also try out various versions on the computer before arriving at this profile view.

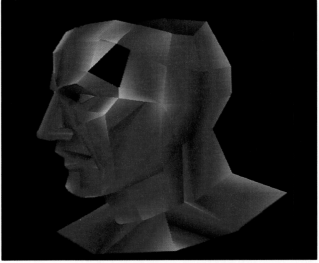

After sketching the outline, it is a simple matter to fill in the planes, using the shading function described on pages 46–47. To see more clearly how this is done, look at the next two details.

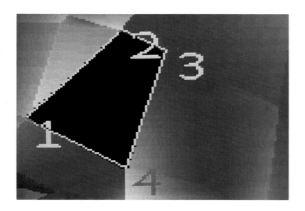

In this detail you can see the rubberband figure—the quadrangle—in position, ready to be filled in. The numbers identify the four corners, into each of which you place a color. The computer then shades the quadrangle automatically.

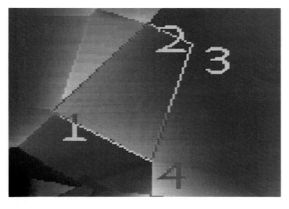

Now the area has been shaded. Note that the rubberband figure usually disappears when the color appears—it has been left here only to clarify the sequence.

Below

Making an image work on a computer presents the same difficulties as in any other medium—it's not a simple step-by-step procedure. In this case, once the basic image is down, I experiment with different effects. Here, for example, I play with the background color. The wonderful thing is that if I don't like what happens, I can always go back to my original—something that's almost impossible with traditional illustration media.

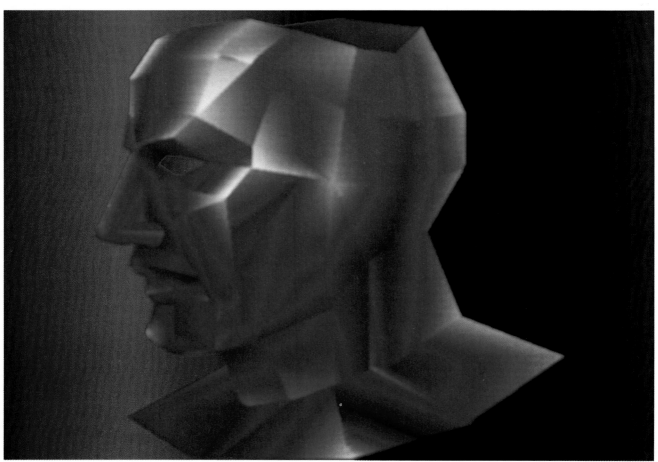

At this point I decide to do a frontal view of the head. Using the automatic line function, I first draw the horizontal lines as guide-lines to help me translate the side view into a frontal outline. Unfortunately, the actual translation process is not automatic—that is not a characteristic of two-dimensional systems. The profile view serves as a reference point, but essentially I have to redraw the frontal view.

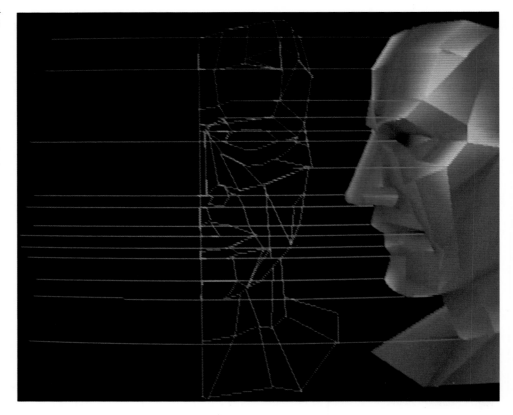

I only have to draw half of the head, however. With the computer I can then mirror the right half to get the left half. This kind of copying function obviously saves a lot of time, as well as boredom. You can then go in and modify details if you don't want everything to be exactly symmetrical.

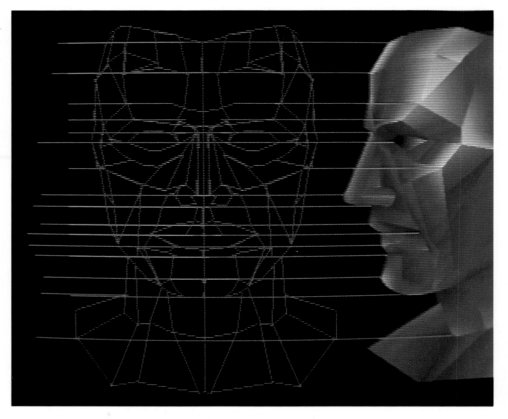

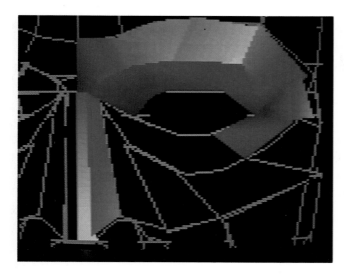

This detail shows the panels being filled in with the shading function, much as in the profile view. The jagged lines characteristic of this painting system are quite evident in this closeup. Although this effect could be lessened with a fuller palette (and thus a much closer range of values), it is hard to avoid entirely. Here, however, it seems appropriate to the robot-like subject.

It is only necessary to shade half the head, as once again it can be mirrored to create the whole. Modifications, however, are in order—as shown on the next page—because lighting in this case must be modulated, much as in traditional illustration.

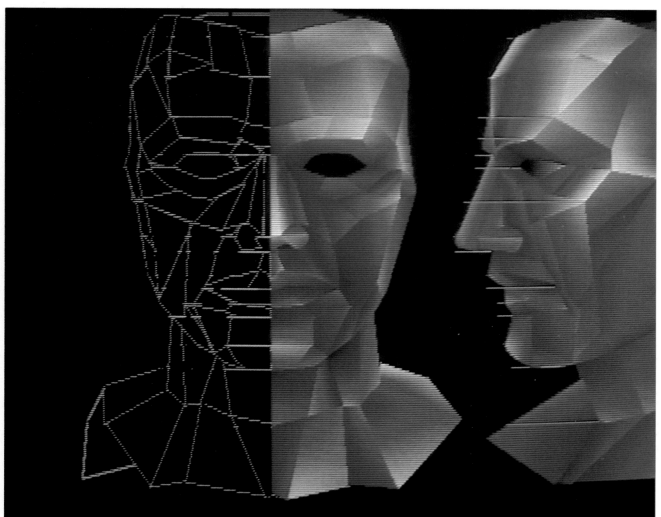

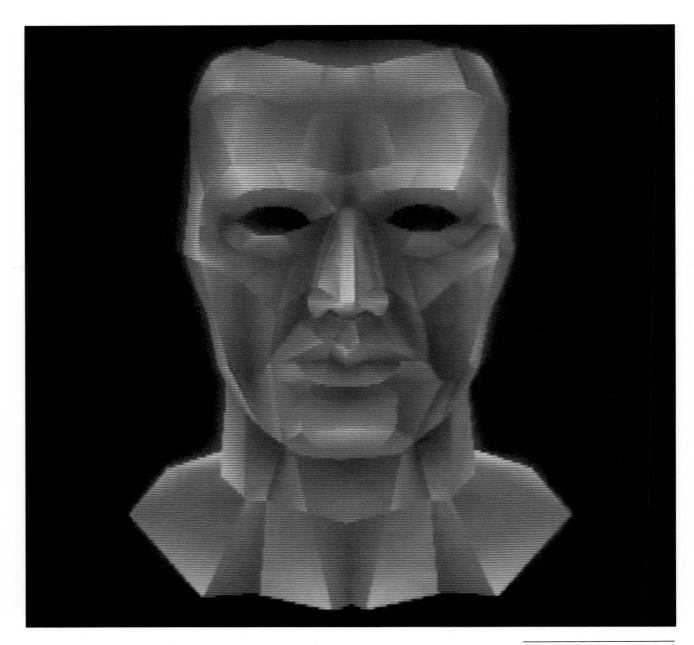

This is the final image, after adjustments to unify the lighting. If you look carefully at the two halves of the head, you can see they're not exact mirror images. There are subtle differences—around the eyes, for example, or the side of the neck—which keep this head from being perfectly symmetrical and thus add some life to it.

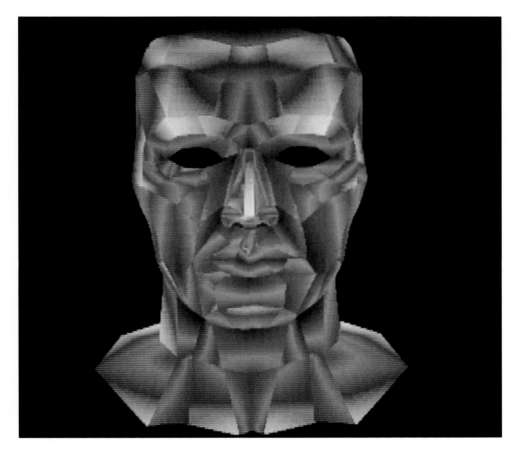

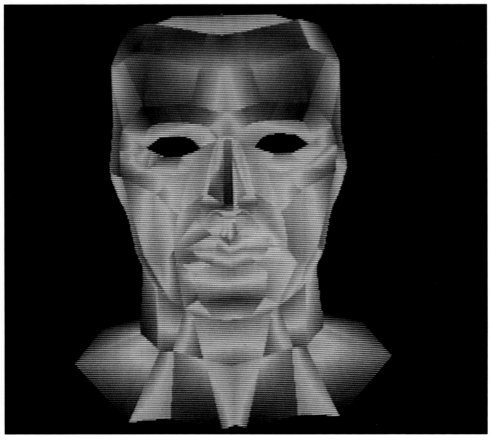

These two images show how easy it is to explore different color variations on the computer. But it isn't just the color that has changed; the position of darks and lights on the palette was also reversed— making for a different dramatic effect.

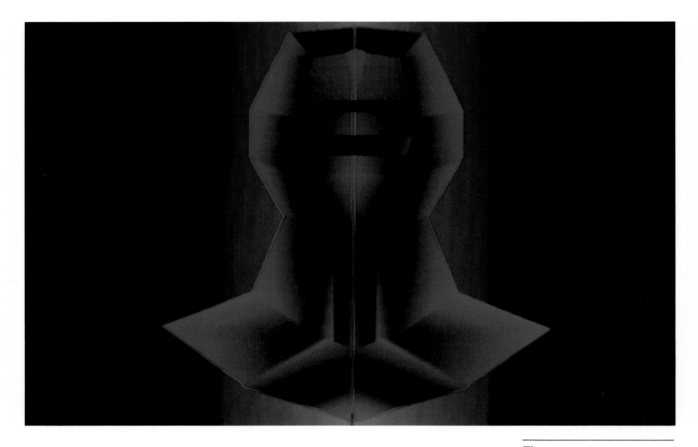

The computer encourages playfulness because it's so easy to generate new images. This armored knight was made by using the back half of the profile view of the android (see the bottom figure on page 51). This back half was then mirrored and the images joined with two horizontal bars . . . and the new picture was complete.

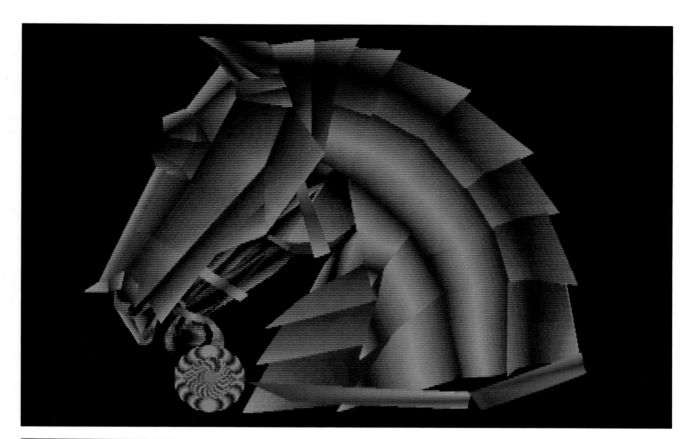

*To my mind, no knight is
complete without a horse to
joust from. I thus went on to
create the horse you see
here, using an essentially
similar technique. Notice, in
particular, how I've made
use of the bending ca-
pability of the shading function in describing the
convex forms.*

MANIPULATING THE IMAGE

One of the functions that eased the making of the android and the armored knight (just shown) was the copying function. As noted in the beginning of this chapter, computer graphics software offers a range of image-enhancing functions that are usually supplied by outside stat houses or photo labs. In addition to copying and mirroring, you can enlarge or reduce an image. You can also rotate it in different directions or "stretch" it horizontally or vertically, changing its shape. The computer thus encourages you to play with the image and to experiment with all kinds of permutations.

Yet another possibility is to start by scanning a photograph or live object in and then solarize or posterize the image, creating a new design configuration. If the image is black and white, you can add color, or vice versa. The excitement of the computer is that it puts all these design possibilities at your fingertips—at no extra cost. You no longer have to wonder what something would look like if you did this or that; you can try it out before your eyes, with hardly any extra work.

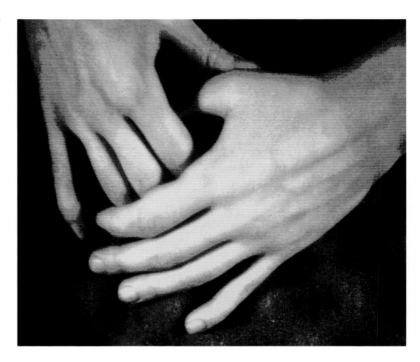

With a scanner, it's possible to input a "live" image such as these hands. You can then manipulate the image in any way you choose, in the same way that you might rework a photograph that you scanned in.

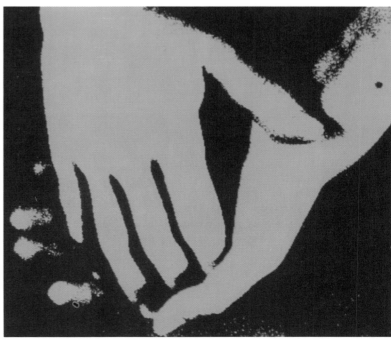

Here—using a slightly different "shot" of the hands—I've increased the graphic impact by posterizing the image. The two colors in this image could easily be changed, again altering the impact.

This car was actually drawn on the computer, although a photo could have been scanned in. As you can see in these two pictures, not only does the computer allow you to alter the color scheme easily, but it enables you to blow up a particular area, so you can work on tiny details. This capacity of quick enlargement makes both designing and retouching easier.

ON SCANNERS

Ask a graphic designer to name his or her tools of the trade and high on the list will be a "swipe file," with "available" photos, illustrations, type styles, and the like. Traditionally, these old images have been incorporated into the new with stats and other photographic means. But computer scanners offer a different possibility.

Essentially, there are two types of color scanning with the computer: pseudo-color and true-color. Pseudo-color scanning allows an image to be broken down into 256 colors, so the results only approximate the original color of the scanned image. Thus, it is best used if the scanned image's color is not a factor, or if the designer intends to redesign the image's color scheme. True-color scanning, on the other hand, attempts to capture all the color nuances in a color photo or live image. It requires a system that can display 16.7 million colors at one time.

The early scanning systems were very expensive and uneven in performance. These two drawbacks may have discouraged many designers from seriously considering the computer as a design tool. Today that has changed. Desktop publishing has spurred the development of relatively inexpensive black-and-white scanners, which now provide much of what stats have always provided for the designer. And these one-color scanners can be purchased as peripherals, off the shelf, and added on to a system—making them more affordable. (Previously scanning equipment could be purchased only from a vendor of the computer graphics system, which always resulted in a higher price.)

Full-color scanning, however, is still tied to specific graphics boards and software and must be purchased through the maker of the paint system. It is expensive, but the prices reflect the general downward course of the cost of all computer graphics systems.

PART TWO

TWO-DIMENSIONAL APPLICATIONS

MEMO
11/28   7:23 A.M.

From: R. T. Stonewall, President
            One Stop Computers, Inc.
To: M. R. Jackson, Account Executive
            Smart Guys Advertising, Inc.
Re: New plug for applications

Applications—that's one of our strong points. Think about it this way: What do agencies need yesterday to show their clients? What has to look slick, but be done super-fast, only to be done again? In a word, Ms. Jackson, C-O-M-P-S. And what gets that job done? One Stop, of course. I want a storyboard on that theme—fast!

MEMO
11/28   1:59 P.M.

From: M. R. Jackson, Account Executive
            Smart Guys Advertising, Inc.
To: R. T. Stonewall, President
            One Stop Computers, Inc.

You're right, R. T. And who should know how right better than us? Our storyboard idea is simply a day in the life of an ad agency—the kind of day you couldn't survive without a One Stop computer graphics workstation. The ad will be live-action. For the art buyer, we'd like to use an actor who specializes in "fast talk." The designer will barely get a word in. A sample script is enclosed. Hope you like it.

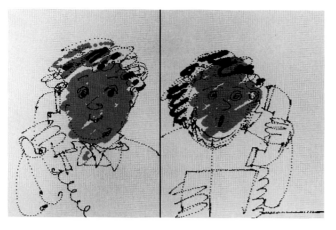
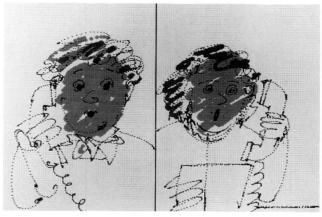
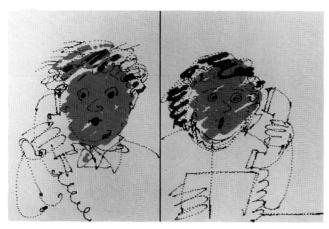

(SCRIPT)

The phone rings.

Art Buyer (urgently): Hello, is this Computer Comp Studio?

Designer: Yes, what . . .

Art Buyer (interrupting): This is Anne Ryan, art buyer for ABC Advertising. I think we may have a job for you. Are you available now?

Designer: I think . . .

Art Buyer (interrupting): Good. It's a real rush job. You say on your card that "Computer graphics can produce finished-looking comps faster than traditional techniques." That's just what we need. Our agency is pitching a new account and the presentation is in 72 hours. Do you think you can do it?

Designer: How much work are . . .

Art Buyer (interrupting): The creative director wants to present three different approaches, with three or four ideas for each approach. We're talking between nine and twelve finished comps. Of course, that's after we get the concepts finalized. We want to talk to you about that, too. Can you come in at noon today?

Designer: No prob– . . .

Art Buyer (interrupting yet again): The art directors here want to know what your computer can do. Bring a lot of samples of your work—slides and print samples, plus a reel, because the agency wants to introduce the presentation with an AV sequence featuring the product. We'll explain it when you come in. I'm on the ninth floor, OK? See you.

The phone still in his hand, the designer reaches out with relief to embrace the monitor of his One Stop computer graphics workstation.

Enter command

Enter command

The cursor blinks.

LEON-
ARDO
DA
VINCI

COMPS

In the movie *All That Jazz* there is a scene, repeated at intervals, in which a red-eyed director, just waking up, looks in a mirror. In anticipation of another grueling day of rehearsal and rewriting, he raises his hands and says mockingly, "It'ssss showtime." That scene epitomizes the state in which creative artists so often find themselves: at the center of chaos. But computer graphics, with its ability to produce quick permutations of an idea, may provide some relief.

Comps, as all commercial artists know, are an essential link in the visual communication chain. They illuminate an idea, allowing all concerned to see if it will be viable in graphic form. And computer graphics, as this chapter illustrates, is an ideal comping tool.

Faced with a tight deadline, a designer can rapidly work up several sketches with both color and compositional variations. Slides or prints can then be quickly made, or the client can be invited to see the work directly on the monitor in the studio. To traditionally trained artists, the idea of an art director looking over your shoulder and making constant (often contradictory) suggestions may sound like a nightmare. But the computer, with its interactive capabilities, creates a positive collaborative atmosphere. The artist doesn't have to worry about losing the original, while the client can immediately see the effect of suggested color and design changes.

This comp for a book jacket puts the lettering function and the averaging function (see page 43) to use. Note that it's relatively easy to change the position or scale of these elements on the computer.

DEVELOPING AN AGENCY PRESENTATION

The cartoon on page 61 might well have been a prelude for the job shown here. The agency was trying to land a new client—a group that produced helicopters for the defense department—and they wanted a variety of slides, showing diverse advertising approaches.

After discussing the project in detail, the agency left me with a thick folder containing quickly scrawled pencil sketches, lots of notes, and some swipe material. From this I was to provide color sketches of the basic concepts, finished comps, and finally a batch of illustrations for an audiovisual presentation.

The beginning wasn't easy. Artists from time immemorial have stared at the blank page or newly stretched canvas and pondered the first move. A blank computer monitor is no less intimidating. Fortunately, in this instance, I at least had the agency sketches.

I started sketching with standard computer brushes and flat colors— a fast and direct technique, much like working with markers, but with the added advantage of allowing quick color changes. I did dozens of sketches, storing only those with possibilities. Then I photographed the best directly from the monitor and, within three hours, the slides were at the agency.

Soon the approved sketches came back and I went to work on the comps, using different techniques to suggest what the ultimate finish would look like. Computer graphics might or might not be used in the final version— that didn't matter at this point. What did matter was the ability to quickly produce finished comps and slides. All the material—more than a hundred slides including finished comps and slides for audiovisual presentation—was delivered within the initial deadline of four days.

This approach, aimed at various government officials, was to show the contractors as America's "first" team—what might be called a flag-waving approach. Here you can see how the White House and the statue on top were created as isolated elements. Actually, the windows were also created separately and saved. When the dome was finished, they were called up and placed in position, much as on an overlay. (Note that to do this I had to make the background of the window "cel" a transparent color.) The ability to layer cels in this way is a particular virtue of two-dimensional computer graphics.

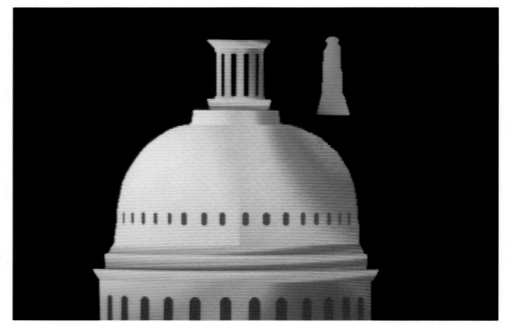

For the background I created another cel—a shaded panel, using the technique described on page 46, which gives the feeling of a dramatic sunset.

On the computer it's easy to combine elements from different cels in one picture. Notice the blank space on the right, which allows type to be added easily to the layout. Before I even began these sketches, I designed a standard format (a blue outline box) to remind me where to leave space for type. I then called this up whenever I started work on a new idea.

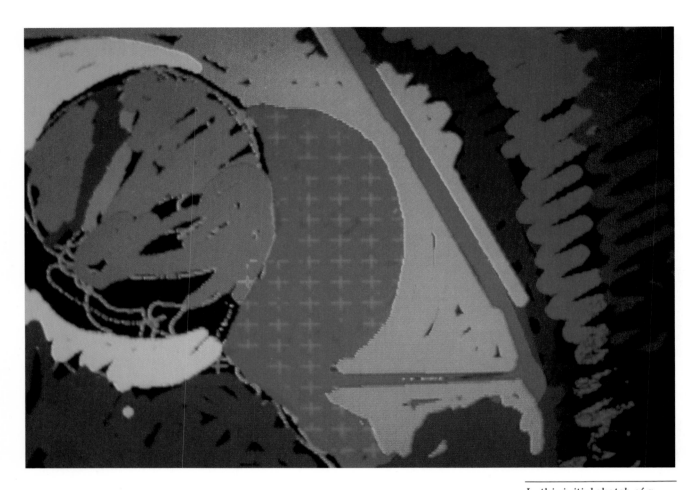

In this initial sketch of a helmeted pilot you can see how the computer can imitate a marker technique. To get this effect I used relatively large dot brushes and drew in the freehand mode. It's important to realize that computer graphics can be just as "loose" as sketches in other media—it all depends on how you use the tools at your disposal.

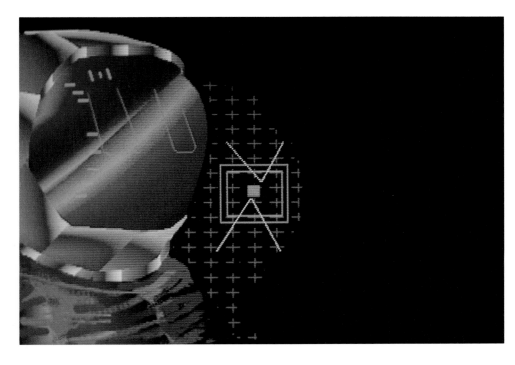

Here the image becomes more concrete. The idea was to show a helicopter pilot with his technological "shadow pilot" (an instrument that acted as a co-pilot and had a range finder built inside its "head"). Notice how the shading and the opaque details create the illusion of a glass visor.

Once again a layering technique was used to create the final image, with the subject from the previous figure saved and layered on top of a shaded background. Of course, the background colors—or any of the other colors—could easily be changed for different effect. The image could also be easily reduced or enlarged.

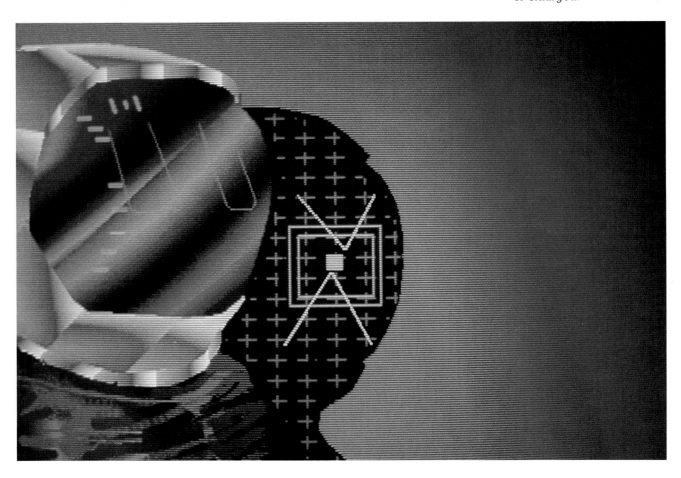

These quick sketches were my first attempts to clarify another one of the agency's concepts. It's similar to the way I might flesh out an idea in a notebook. Used in this way, the computer becomes an electronic sketchbook.

In the final image you can see more clearly the concept of preserving the American way of life and defending our freedoms (symbolized by the kite). Here the figure and the foreground were created as a separate cel and layered on top of the sunset.

This initial sketch and finished comp show a different version of the flag-waving approach. The sixteen stars highlight the participation of sixteen different companies in the development of the helicopter system. The stars, by the way, were made with a star picture brush.

Here the emphasis is on technological innovation. The illustration offers an interpretation of fiber optics, a communications technology to be used in the development of the helicopter. To create this image it was only necessary to do one of the multicolored filaments. This image was then copied and rotated into various positions.

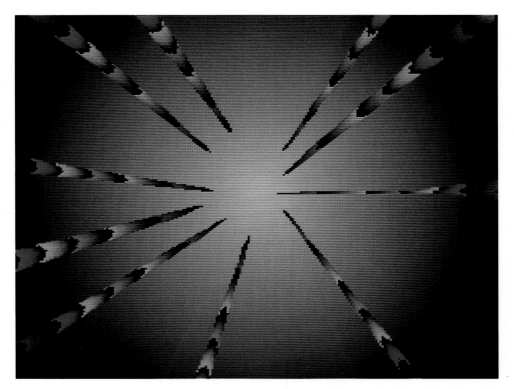

Again, the emphasis is on technological innovation, with a blowup of an instrument panel. This design was easy to do, using the simplest functions of the paint program.

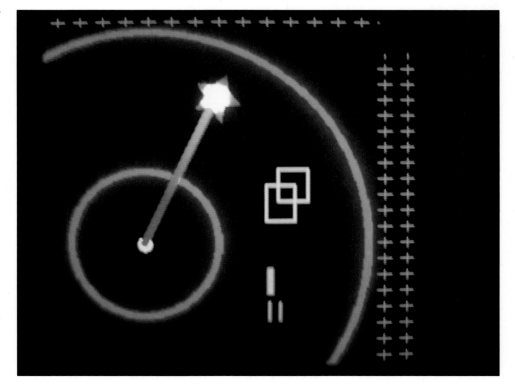

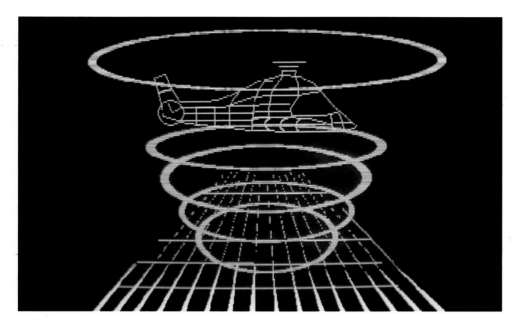

This illustration offers a different symbolic portrayal of the sixteen companies collaborating in the development of the helicopter system. Here the helicopter is taking off from a launching pad made up of sixteen strips. Again, the design uses relatively simple computer drawing functions.

In this final example you see the full comp with the type added. In this case, the image is a new helmet visor, with weapon systems automatically keyed to wherever the eyes look. In many ways the computer seems ideally suited to portraying such technological concepts.

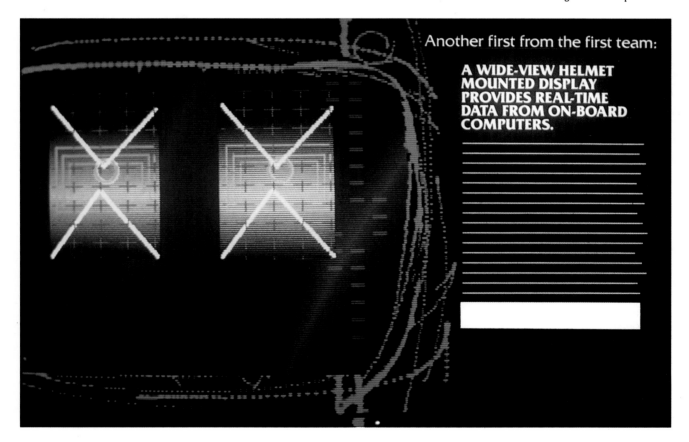

Another first from the first team:

A WIDE-VIEW HELMET MOUNTED DISPLAY PROVIDES REAL-TIME DATA FROM ON-BOARD COMPUTERS.

PROPOSING AN ANNUAL REPORT COVER

Using the computer as a comping tool can be particularly helpful when clients are confused about what they want. A perfect example was provided by a corporation board that couldn't decide on a cover for its annual report. Like a celebrity going out to face the public, the corporation was extremely sensitive about how it looked to its stockholders. The cover therefore began to take on almost cosmic importance. Add an impending deadline, and it was a situation that begged for computer graphics input.

A little client background is necessary here. My colleague and I were told that the corporate conglomerate in question had six companies, each of which provided a technologically oriented product or service. The one other piece of information was that the chairman of the board wanted the cover to reflect a recent upturn in the corporation's financial picture. The idea of advanced technology, the number "six," and financial optimism thus became the basic abstractions underlying the design effort.

Juggling elements, playing with various combinations, and eventually deciding on the best is the way designers usually arrive at their solutions. Designing at a computer graphics workstation is no different. In this case, we began by selecting six basic colors (one for each company). Using a variety of tools, we created several multi-colored symbols, some of which were later made into picture brushes. We also played with graphs (the financial theme) and different metallic, machine-like effects.

The ability to custom-design a picture brush and the related functions of pattern making, picture averaging, and paint pushing deserve special mention here. These tools can give a shot of adrenalin to a flagging imagination. Designing

(especially under a deadline) can be exhausting and exhilarating by turns, and a tool capable of producing "lucky accidents" can rescue a designer just when he or she is approaching burnout.

Another important tool in carrying out our explorations was the save function. At the initial stages of a design's development, there are so many paths to follow that it's easy to lose track of promising leads. By saving bits and pieces of experiments, either as images or patterns, you can pursue an early idea later, in a different context, perhaps with a different palette. Sometimes, working with computer graphics, a designer may go through so many revisions that he or she would have filled up a couple of flat files if the work had been done in traditional media.

The excitement generated by working in this way with computer graphics was borne out by a visit from one of the corporate vice-presidents. As he sat in front of the monitor, seeing idea after idea turn into an image, a change came over him. His studied speech became animated, and sentences that began as corporate jargon ended with allusions to graphic symbols. After an hour or so he was scribbling on a large pad. Happily none of this ad-lib designing was offered as a solution; it was more an act of self-discovery—or perhaps the rediscovery of an imagination dormant for years. Later it was reported that the vice-president, on returning to his office, borrowed a set of markers and a pad and disappeared for the rest of the day.

In the end, more than a hundred slides, representing variations of a half-dozen basic themes, were submitted for consideration. But then, under threat of a hostile takeover, the management decided to use a straightforward typographic cover, featuring the latest financial highpoints. Well, that's the design business.

These initial sketches were done quickly using a multi-colored picture brush and the automatic curve function. The six different colors (or companies) work together in a single image, with the upward sweep of the curve suggesting a financial upturn. These images were saved, so they could easily be reused later, on different backgrounds and with different colors.

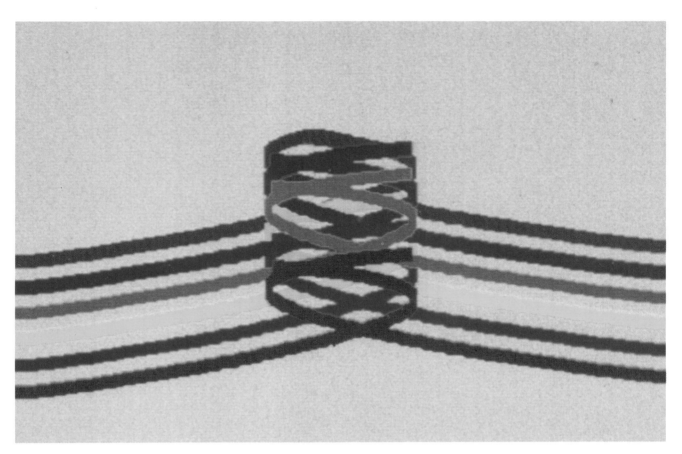

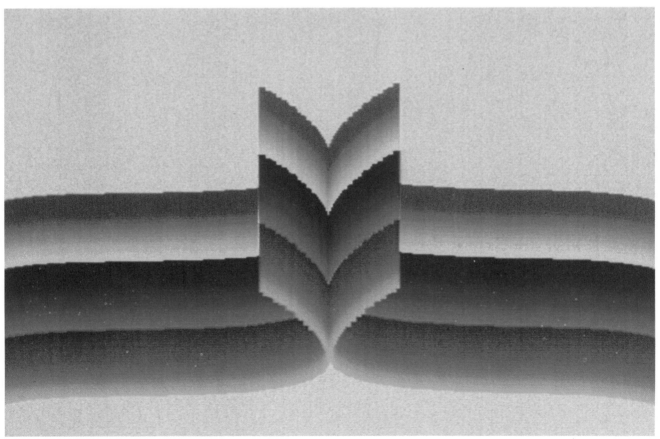

This image uses the automatic shading function, described on page 46, within the six elongated quadrilaterals. The two greens become almost mirror-image reversals simply by changing the color in the corner points.

This rectangle was also automatically shaded, but here the palette had colors going to white, creating the separations you see between colors.

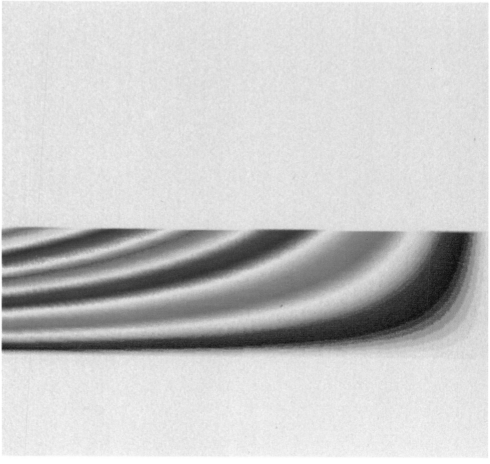

These two designs are variations of the first image on this spread, with the addition of a grid behind or in front. Different color possibilities were tested by using the color-cycling function, much as in the letterforms on page 45. This process can be an eye-opener, suggesting combinations the artist might not have arrived at otherwise.

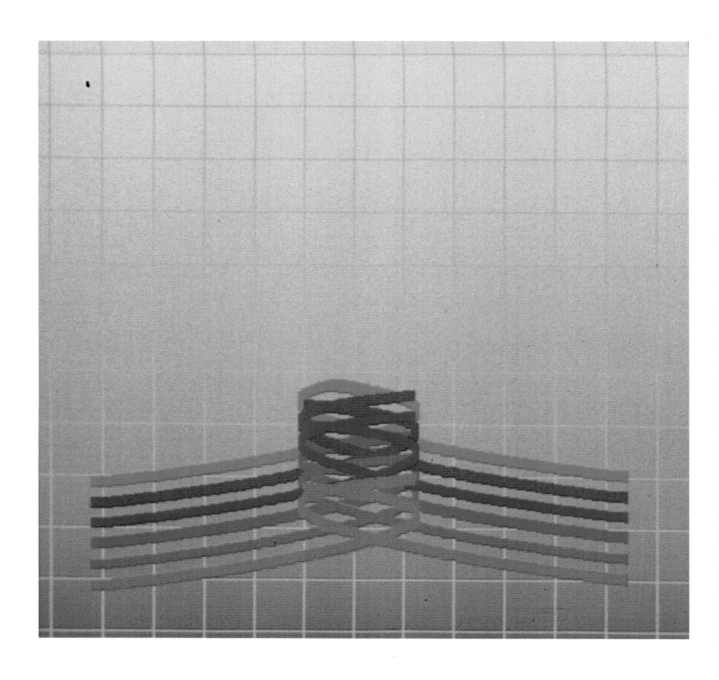

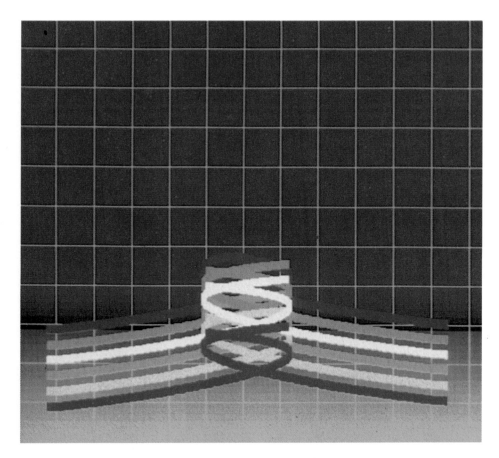

These three designs clearly
show the computer's advantage in being able to
quickly present permuta-
tions of the same idea.
Changes like these take
minutes, rather than hours,
and you can save each new
version as an original.

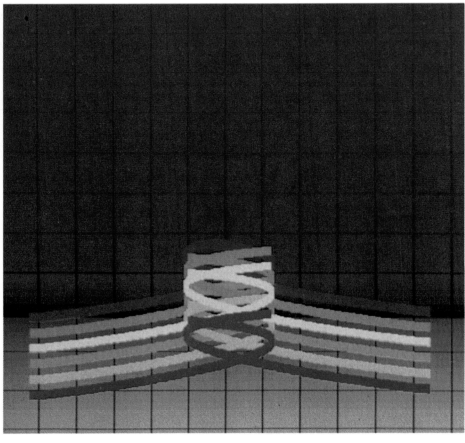

Another six-color picture brush was used with the automatic line function to create this design. Other variations (not shown here) enlarged this image and repositioned it—moving it, for example, to the top of the page. Instead of wondering, "What if . . ." on a computer you can quickly try it out.

The same picture brush was used here, but in a clear upward movement to suggest economic growth.

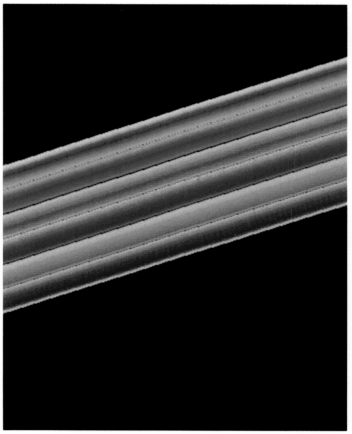

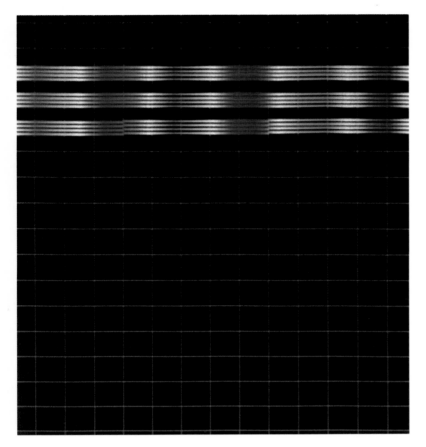

This image uses a somewhat different technique. After first creating a multicolored, horizontal rectangle, we overlaid it with a black mask, leaving the horizontal line pattern you now see.

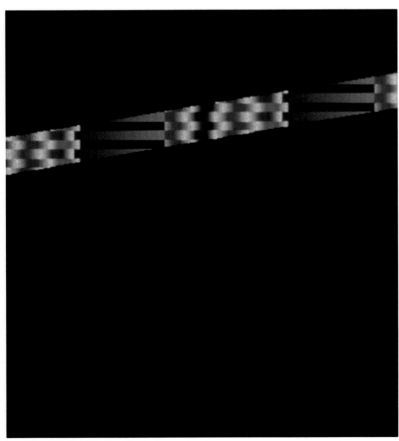

This design gives more emphasis to the technological products and services of the corporation. There's a sense of looking at the innards of gleaming metal machinery. The particular pattern, with its suggestion of meshing gears, was arrived at by chance, in the process of playing around with different ideas. It was one of those "happy accidents" that are such a great benefit of computer graphics. And it ended up being both our and the corporate art director's favorite design.

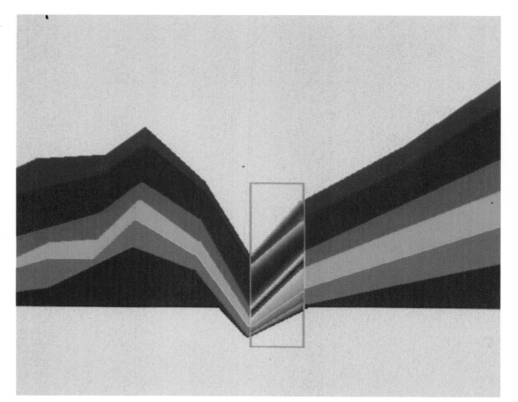

This image is an attempt to combine the idea of six companies (or colors) with a financial graph showing the past, present, and future economic profits of the corporation. The small vertical rectangle in the center represents the year covered in the annual report.

Adding shading in this way and brightening the colors in the center increase the dynamic feeling of the graph. On the facing page, the image has simply been reduced and incorporated into the format of the actual annual report cover.

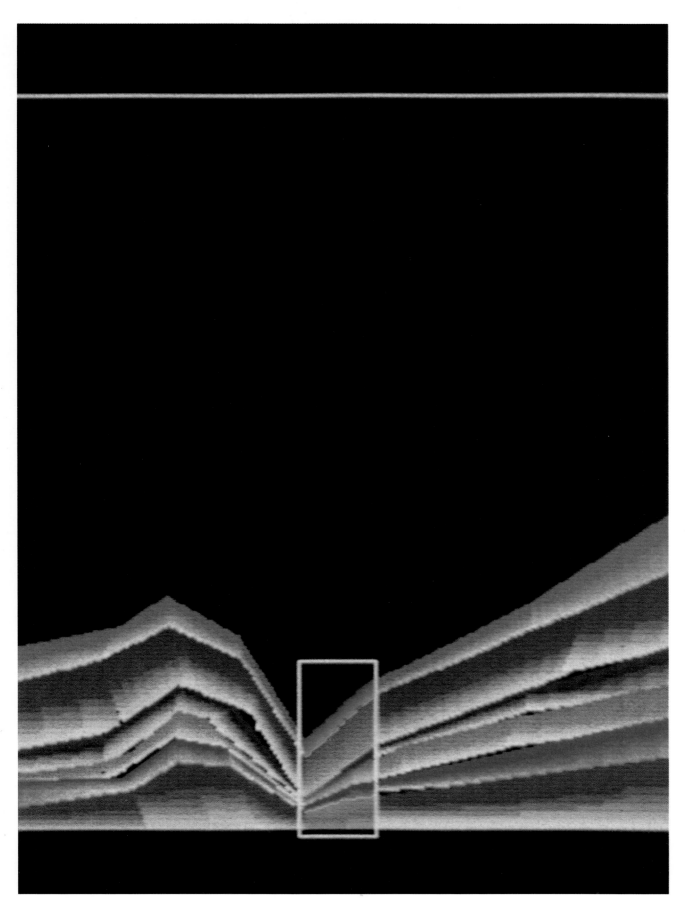

FINISHED ART

Pixel resolution, or the presence of "jaggies," is not a problem at the comp stage. If, however, an image from a typical computer paint system is headed for print reproduction, the issue of pixel visibility must be addressed. Both the artist and the client should analyze the suitability of computer graphics to the job in question—at least at the moment. In the future this issue should disappear. Already some computer paint systems have reduced jaggies as a factor, although at present these systems are either unwieldy (creatively speaking) or very expensive.

The point to keep in mind is that full-color, computer-generated printed matter is beginning to appear in advertising and mass-market books and magazines, not just desktop publications. For now, due to the pixel-related limitations, most art directors feel that the subject matter must in some way relate to computers or advanced technology for computer graphics to be used. But there is the flip side to that coin. A company with a high-tech product, for example, might well see computer graphics as an ideal way of underlining its technological character.

Even though a lot of the subject matter for finished computer art is high-tech, an image as playful as this could find its way into a children's book. For other examples of children's book illustrations, see pages 91–97.

That computer graphics can actually help highlight new technology is demonstrated by the ad on the following pages. The assignment was to create an ad for a new, computer-controlled system to monitor the location of various armed forces around the world. When we discussed the possibility of doing the finished art on a computer, the art director said, "Jaggies are no problem. In fact, the client wants to emphasize the system's computer aspect."

"That's great," I replied. "But what about the hand?" I asked, pointing to the comp.

The art director agreed that that was a concern, that the client wanted a clear contrast between the computer elements and the hand. I then assured her that I could do this with computer techniques or, if necessary, by combining the ad with a traditionally rendered hand. (As it turned out, I was able to do it with computer techniques alone, but more on that later.)

Using my comp as a guide, I first established the appropriate trim size, with room for the type. The next step was the creation and organization of my palette. Initially I concentrated on three areas: the large tabletop filling the bottom two-thirds of the page, the night

sky at the top, and the hand. Each of these areas required enough colors to produce a smooth, gradated tone. After assigning 64 colors to the tabletop, 64 to the hand, and 32 to the sky, I still had plenty of colors left for the symbols and the grid.

In this case my computer-painting technique resembled collage or printmaking, in that elements were layered one upon the other to form the complete composition. The hand, symbols, and grid, for example, were all created before the tabletop and sky.

A distinct advantage of the computer here is that various elements, such as the hand or symbols, can be done separately, saved as silhouettes, and later be recalled onto any surface—giving you a lot of design flexibility. Here I changed some of the symbol shapes, reversed their colors, and shifted their positions as I worked. The tonal areas also underwent several transformations.

At one point I departed radically from the comp by trying out a black background under the grid. I liked the results so much that I decided to include a slide of this with the approved version. Agreeing that it was an exciting alternative, the art director pleaded for an opportunity to let the client de-

cide. The account director was reluctant (why press one's luck?), but the art director carried the day. And, to everyone's surprise, the client liked it.

But what about the finished art? What form did it take? Here we come to an advance that is signaling far-reaching changes in the print industry. Earlier it had been decided that the finished piece would be prepared as either a 4×5 or 35mm transparency using a digital film recorder. The color separations would then be made from the chrome. While working on the project, however, I learned of a method of preparing four-color separations directly from a floppy disk, thereby eliminating the photographic step altogether. The method is simple: digital information (in this case, the image) is transformed from the disk to magnetic tape, using a program that allows the data to be read by the Scitex four-color separation process. The resulting image is identical to the original because it is made from the same data. And picture fidelity is not the only benefit: this method is less costly than traditional photographic methods. Eventually the lower production costs of this full-color process will expand the use of color in the publishing industry.

This hand was created using the same shading function as the head of the android on pages 50–55. The difference lies in the arrangement of the color palette, with a subtler range of colors, which minimizes the hard-edge, robot-like quality of the android. Note the contrast between the warm flesh tone and the bluish light on the back of the hand. I liked this effect, but the client didn't—too theatrical, perhaps.

These outlined, toy-like figures symbolize the opposing armed forces. Notice how the shading suggests lighting from below. Also notice the greater pixel visibility, giving a more computer-made look to the symbols than the hand.

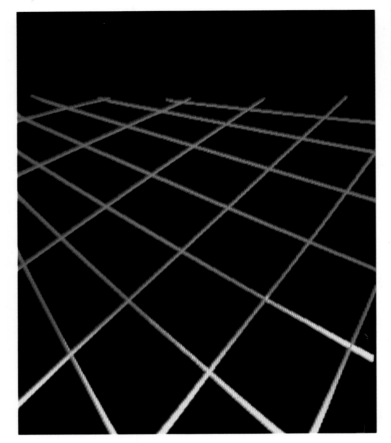

This grid was saved as a separate cel. Notice that the upper part is only one color, while the foreground section uses very thin shaded areas to set up the light-dark contrast.

This background cel was done last. Although the tabletop in front may look simple, it required a relatively large palette to achieve the smooth gradations you see here. It may be surprising, but the palette for the night sky has only half as many colors.

Right

After doing the separate cel of the hand shown on page 85, I made a new cel, combining the hand with certain symbols. Obviously, the hand and the missile had to be done as one piece. Adding the soldier was a matter of convenience, ensuring that these elements would always be in the same relationship.

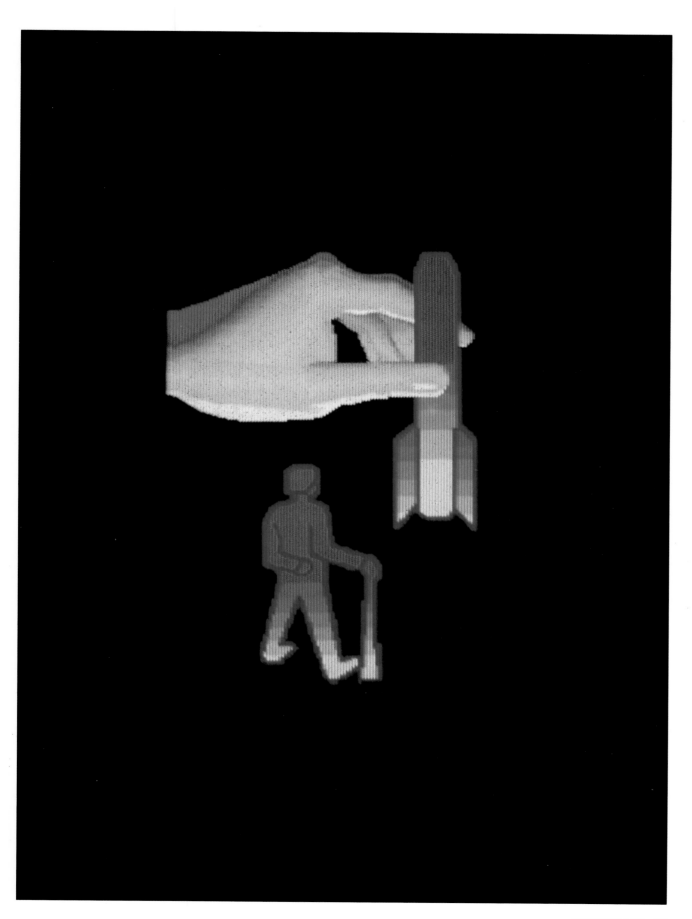

Once all the cels—the hand, the symbols, the grid, and the background—were complete, I layered them to create the total picture. At this point it was still possible to make adjustments in the color and even the position of the elements—something that would have been much more difficult in traditional media. In one variation (not shown here) I tried a little less yellow in the tabletop and more red in the horizon.

Here you see the decided advantage of the computer in allowing major changes, with almost no headaches, up to the last minute. The whole background color scheme has been drastically altered. The foreground grid has also been darkened. Moreover, the colors of the symbols have been reversed, and one of the symbol shapes has been changed (from a carrier to a destroyer). The net effect of these changes is to focus more interest on the hand, bringing out the human component within the computerized system.

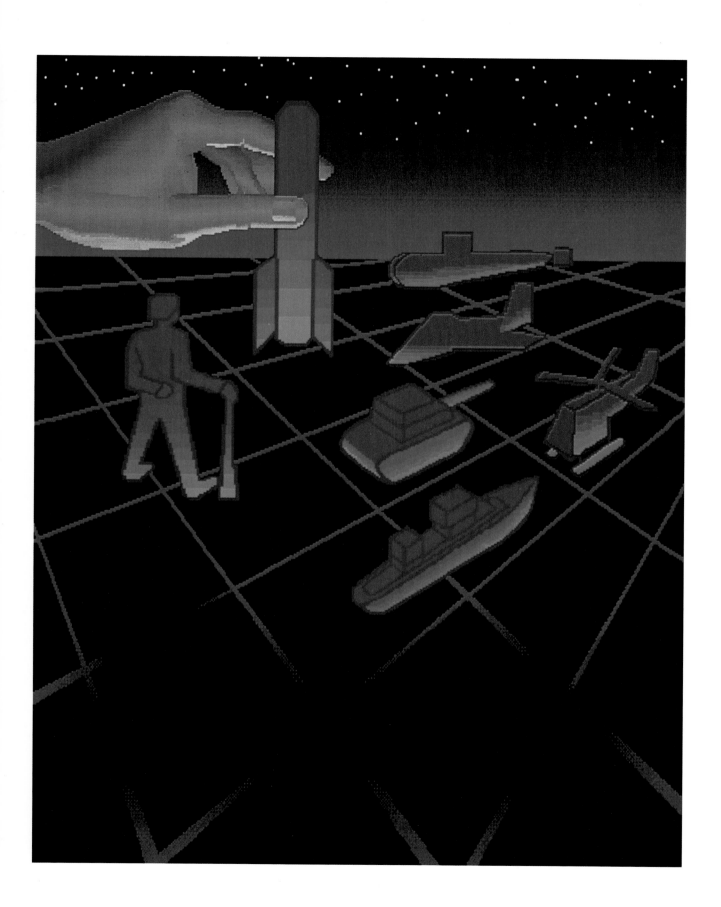

A different example of computer graphics in print comes from book publishing. But, again, the subject and the technique are related.

Anthropomorphism has been a staple of storytelling since the earliest legends and myths. Rabbits, mice, bears, even flowers and vegetables, have acquired human characteristics in the many variations of this theme. The latest variation substitutes machines for the usual furry creature. Computerized, high-tech vehicles may assume a human nature, complete with sibling rivalry and a desire to please and be loved.

At least that was the case in *Maxx Trax II*, a book by James Preller that I illustrated for Scholastic Publications. It was the second book in a series about a family of super-vehicles that work in and watch over a world without humans. And it seemed a natural for computer graphics.

As you can see in the illustrations on the following pages, this project presented opportunities for using almost every feature of the paint menu. Note, in particular, the range of textural contrasts: the hard-edged truck bodies, gleaming fenders, gritty soil, reflective windshields, pulsing lights, and glowing skies. I hope you also get a sense of the fun of computer graphics and the way it can encourage your own creativity and inventiveness.

There are, of course, many other examples of computer graphics in print, ranging in size from posters to postage stamps. Most reflect the point of view that computer graphics is best used for subjects that the viewer associates with computers or advanced technology. Higher-resolution paint programs will certainly reduce objections based on pixel visibility, but new print opportunities for computer graphics will also come as more artists become expert in it, apply its techniques to unexpected subjects, and justify its use aesthetically and economically.

The initial comp for the book jacket was done, for the most part, in a marker-like technique, using a large dot brush and flat color. But, as you can see, there were a lot of changes. The art director wanted the creature in the top half—a "Metallasaur"—to be larger and the title to be more prominent. Even more striking is the change in technique, with the shading function used to create metallic-looking surfaces. The simplification of the color scheme also helps to reinforce the high-tech look.

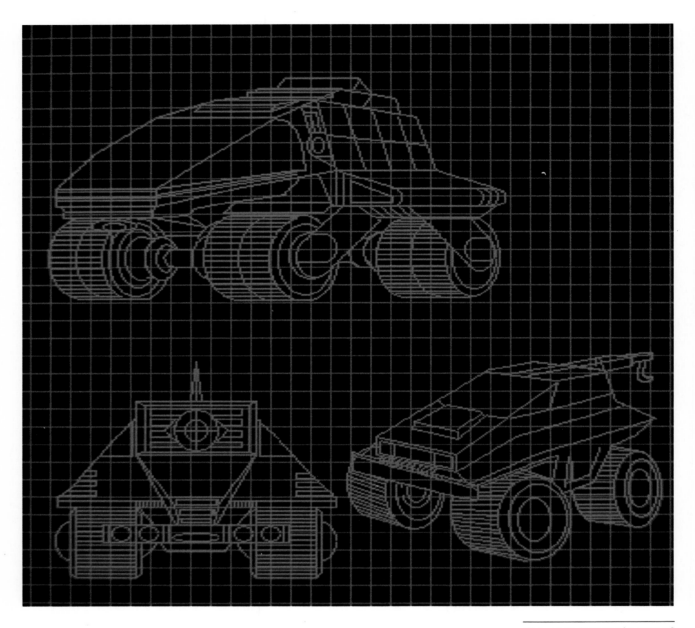

This page is part of a spread used to introduce the characters in the book. Showing these wireframe vehicles on a grid provided a good contrast to the full-color, fully modeled vehicles that follow. Note, however, that these drawings were done on a two-dimensional, not a three-dimensional system, so they could not simply be recalled and rotated to create the other positions seen in the book.

Here you see part of the
Maxx Trax family in operation. This illustration reveals
many of the paint functions
discussed in the chapter on
software. The "push" function, for example, was used
to create the explosion on
the right and the texture on
the rocks on the lower left,
where the wheels go over
them. Geometric shading
helped to create the win-
dows, while cycle painting
suggested the laser beams
that are destroying the
rocks.

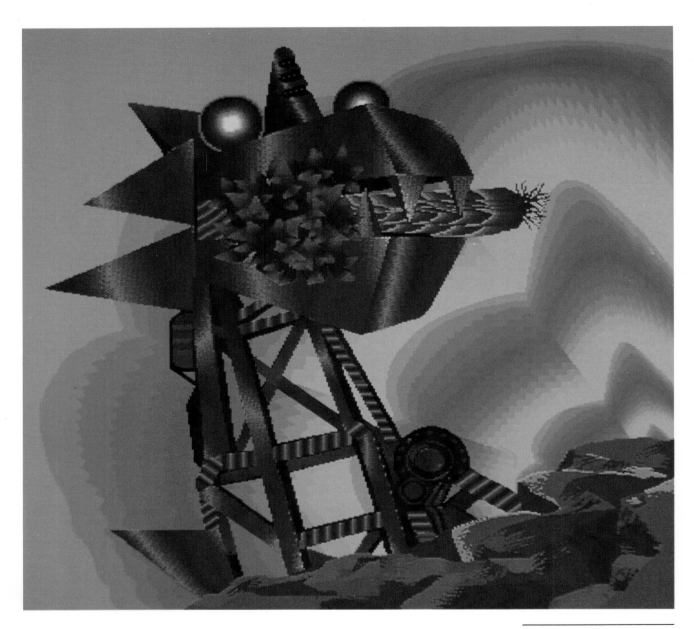

In the background here there are sonar waves, sent out by an evil creature, called a "Draxial." These waves drive the Metallasaur crazy, and in his frenzy he rips out a tree. To suggest the sonar waves, I shaded a large panel and then copied and recopied a section over itself, producing what I call a "lucky accident." For the tree leaves, I used a special picture brush. The Metallasaur was done with a combination of the shading function and cycle painting.

The two youngest members
of the Maxx Trax family—
brother and sister—are
chained to pillars. The pillars are a good example of
how you can create a three-
dimensional look with the
shading function. Also
notice the black panel with
the "flashing" lights in the
background; it was done
with grid alignment and
cycle painting.

Now the evil Draxial and his sidekick "Retread" come out of hiding and are captured. The simple geometric forms seem well-suited to computer graphics treatment. Look closely at the edge of the armor-like surface—again, you can see the effect of cycle painting.

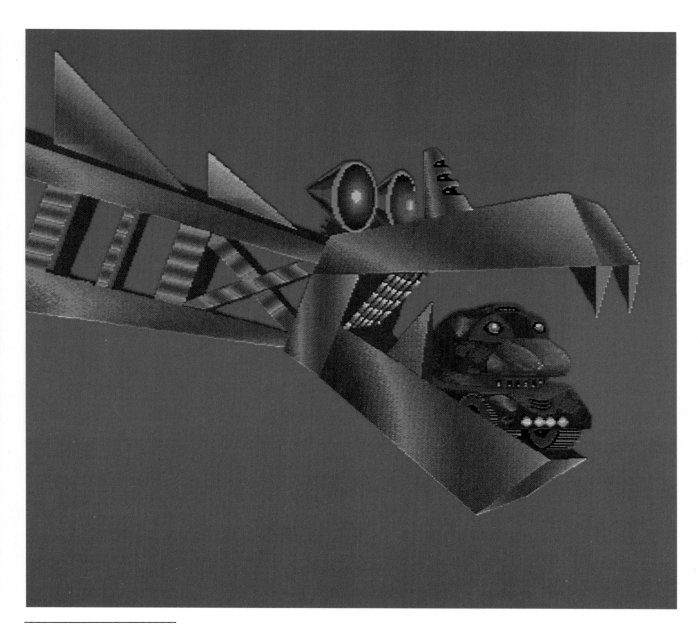

Finally, the bad guys get their comeuppance. The Metallasaur gobbles up the two villains and takes them away to work on repairing the damage they've done. Again, note the combination of shading and cycle painting in the Metallasaur. Look particularly at the mouth; you can almost see the color cycling in the back.

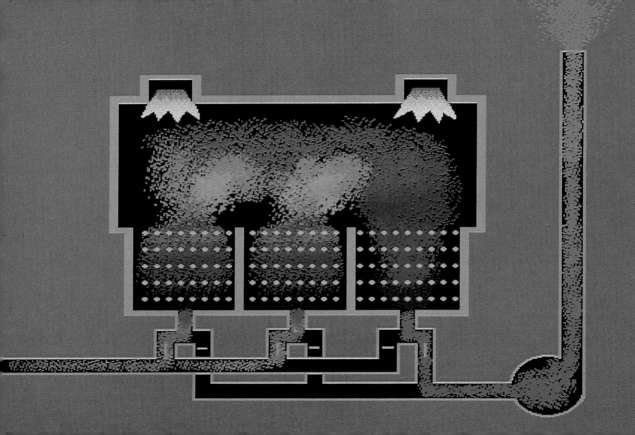

AUDIOVISUAL PRESENTATIONS

Computer graphics is changing the nature of communications within the business world. Slides created by computer paint programs are adding a new, visual dimension to corporate discussions. Colorful graphs of growth and productivity, for example, can easily be prepared and projected to add to the impact of a business presentation. A technical illustration can be thrown in to clarify a particular point, or a humorous spot can be inserted to enliven an otherwise dull chart.

Computer graphics can also become part of a multi-image slide show. Using six, nine, twelve, or more projectors, you can then transfer the slide show to videotape, providing yet another format for the information. In this way it is also possible to produce limited animation effects without inordinate costs.

This image is a frame from a videotape using cycle animation. The idea was to show schematically the operation of a thermal oxidizer, a device used to control air pollution.

PREPARING BUSINESS SLIDES

Business slides represent a large percentage of the work produced on computer graphics systems. Most computer graphics workstations have special programs for business slides, ranging from simple to moderately difficult in their usability. Essentially these programs automatically translate the statistics into appropriate graphs or pie charts. The artist can then "refine" the presentation, deciding on the colors and typeface and perhaps adding a drop shadow for impact.

For the most part, this slide-making software is vector-based, so it produces high-resolution images and type—four to eight times finer than computer paint systems, which are raster-based (for a dis-

cussion of vector- versus raster-based systems, see page 103). The higher resolution is, of course, a major advantage, but it is difficult to paint complicated images with a vector-based system. Some systems with vector-based business graphics thus provide a compatible paint program, and often images from one program can be merged with the other. But there is a catch: the combined image will have two different levels of resolution.

It seems appropriate to add a word here about another computer possibility: in-house typesetting. Incredible as it may sound, about five years ago desktop publishing didn't even exist. Now it's beginning to flood the business and design world. But, again, these

systems are limited in their ability to combine type and full-color illustrations. Only a few systems—very expensive ones—offer full-color paint capability and high-resolution type specifying and setting. To reiterate: although raster-based paint systems usually supply display type that is anti-aliased (blurring the edges to reduce the jaggies), this is sufficient only for some levels of audiovisual presentation, and it is not of adequate quality for print. Vector-based systems, as noted, give you higher resolution, along with many more type styles and sizes, but they are limited on the pictorial end. Still, it's probably only a matter of time before we have the best of both worlds.

These are typical business slides. Statistical information from business software such as Lotus 1-2-3 provides the data, and the graphics program then automatically translates the figures and percentages into graphs or pie charts. The artist's responsibility lies in the selection and placement of the various elements: the colors, type, and special effects, such as drop shadows and gradations. Because the field is highly competitive, slide-making programs must produce slides economically. Artists cannot afford to spend the same time on a business slide as they can on a magazine or ad illustration.

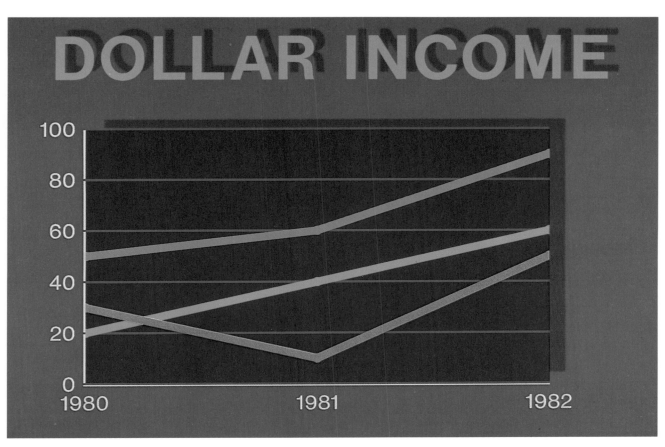

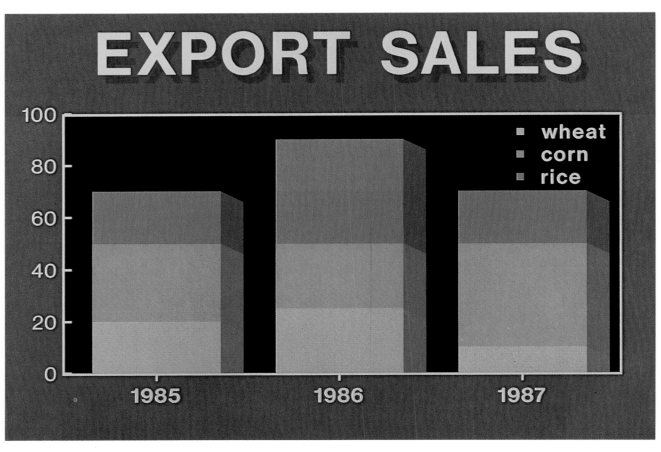

These three figures, all done in Helvetica, show differences in resolution. In the first example—done with a raster-based program—the jaggies have been softened by anti-aliasing (see page 29). The other two examples, both done with vector-based programs, are much sharper. The last, with 4000-line (4k) resolution, is the preferred standard for most corporate presentations.

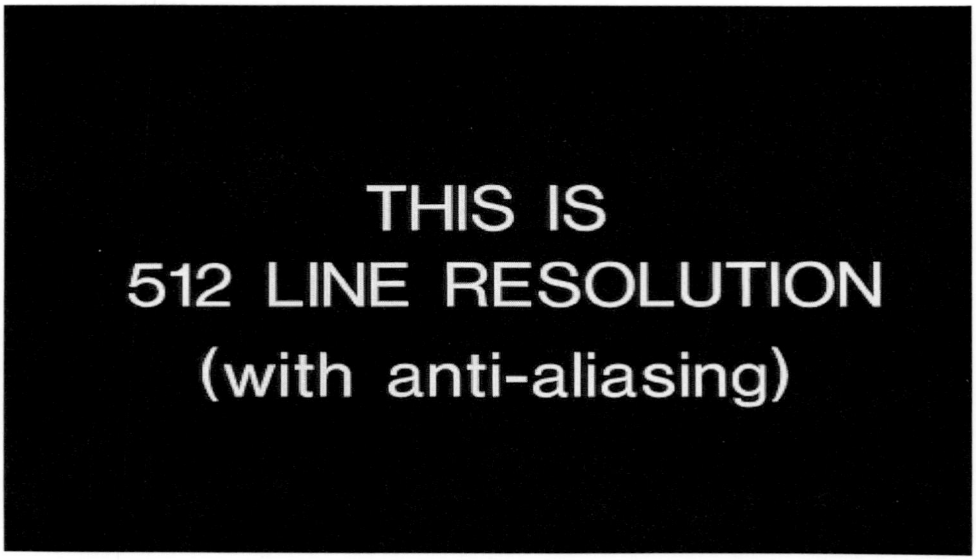

THIS IS
512 LINE RESOLUTION
(with anti-aliasing)

S

THIS IS
2000 LINE RESOLUTION

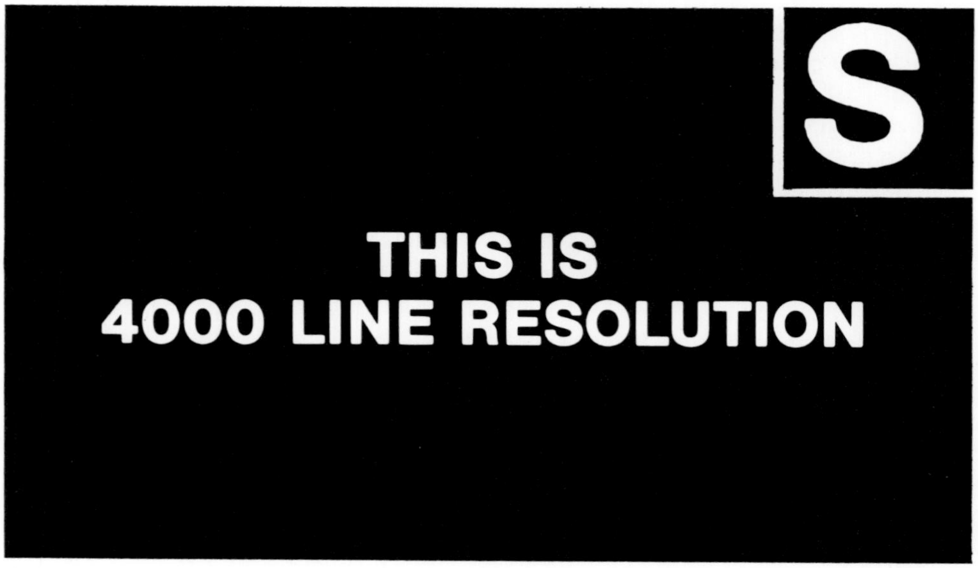

S

THIS IS
4000 LINE RESOLUTION

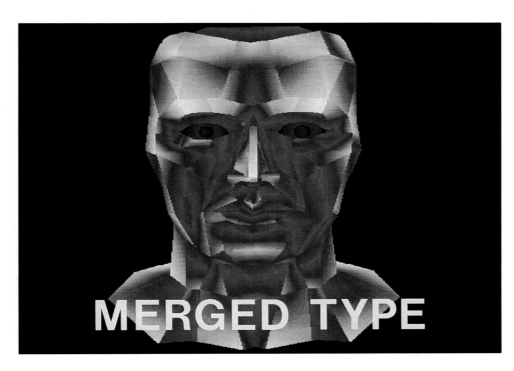

In this merged image, the illustration was done with raster-based (512-line resolution) paint software while the type was done with a vector-based (4k) business slide program. Notice the jaggies that are still evident in the "painted" image. Keep in mind that although with some systems you can see both the illustrations and the type on the monitor at the same time, you can't manipulate them. Making changes thus becomes a somewhat cumbersome process.

RASTER OR VECTOR?

One of the most annoying aspects of new technology is its technical jargon. Computer graphics is no exception. Consider the words "raster" and "vector," which define the two basic types of computer graphics programs.

Paint programs (like the ones used to create most of the color illustrations in this book) are raster-based. These programs allow you to work relatively freely, much as you would with traditional painting techniques. They are also highly interactive and responsive, letting you see what is being painted as it is being painted. The major drawback is the limited resolution: what you see on the monitor is what you will get on a slide or in a printout. This kind of program is called device-dependent.

Vector-based graphics software is, conversely, device-independent. This means that a chart or graph designed with vector-based software may show lots of jaggies on a low-resolution monitor but will have smooth edges when output on a high-resolution film recorder or printer. For this reason, most business graphics programs are vector-based.

What is it like to work with these two types of computer graphics? The differences in approach can be compared to the differences between painting with paint and a brush (raster) and making a collage with scissors and paper (vector). Raster-based programs, like traditional painting, allow for endless repainting and blending of areas; changing one area, however, inevitably affects adjoining areas. In vector-based graphics, as in collage, the areas are discrete and can be changed or removed without affecting other areas in the picture. Subtle alterations of the contours or the tonal areas within the contours can be difficult. Moreover, the interactive responsiveness is not as immediate as with raster-based systems.

The hope of most artists who use raster-based software for illustration is that it will eventually be capable of being imaged at a higher resolution than at present. Artists who use vector-based systems await the day of greater flexibility in their programs. Lately there has been talk of paint programs that combine the best of both—that remains to be seen.

USING LIMITED ANIMATION

It's possible to use some of the computer graphics techniques described in Part One to create animation effects—first producing a slide show and then transferring this to videotape. That, at least, was the process for several animation segments in a training film done for Mercedes-Benz, the car manufacturer. It goes without saying that it was more economical to use computer-generated art than traditional animation.

The film, which was directed toward dealers and their sales personnel, endeavored to explain in lay terms some of the high-tech features of the new models. One segment, for example, dealt with the engineering expertise that went into the making of a comfortable driver's seat. Different sections of the seat were highlighted, with appropriate commentary.

To do this sequence, I first designed the overall illustration of the driver in the seat on the computer; then, after it was approved, I broke it down into its separate components, putting each seat section on a separate slide. For the final slide show I used about eleven or twelve slides and six projectors, so it was possible to carefully control the dissolve time. (Actually the projectors were computer-controlled, programmed to superimpose each component in the proper order.) When everyone (including the client) was satisfied, the sequence was transferred to 1-inch videotape at a post-production facility.

A second sequence (shown on pages 106–107) was more challenging. The problem was to show a moving car coming to an abrupt stop, as well as a standing car suddenly accelerating. The purpose: to demonstrate how Mercedes' unique suspension reduces the "dive" and "squat" tendencies of most cars in these situations.

"Is it possible to convey starting and stopping when the car is standing still?" I wondered. My solution was to use a universal symbol: a speedometer with a moving needle. A moving needle was much easier (and less expensive) to animate than an entire car. And, at the same time, I could still animate the car outline to show a diving front end and a squatting rear end.

For the first showing, I used the same slide-dissolve method as with the car seat sequence. The action, however, wasn't smooth enough to satisfy either me or my client. The solution came in the post-production phase. Using a device called an ADO (Ampex Digital Optics), I was able to get the needle and car to move in a more believable fashion.

The point in all this is that computer graphics can produce limited animation for video that offers a viable alternative to high-priced, classical cel animation. And you don't need highly sophisticated equipment. Most desktop computer graphics workstations are well equipped to provide the necessary artwork.

This sequence shows how each part of the driver's seat provides comfort and support. After an opening "shot" showing the entire seat lit up, the different seat sections are pinpointed, one at a time, in bright orange. The large image here is actually a composite, with a slide of just the orange headrest projected over another slide showing the whole setup. Imagine the headrest slide dissolving as the slide of the seat back (shown below) is projected. Obviously the only thing that really needs to be drawn here is the basic image. The rest is a matter of isolating parts of that image and changing colors.

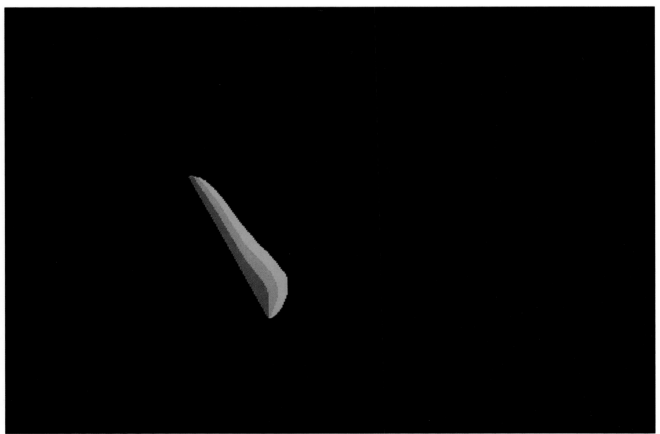

These images are from the "start-and-stop" sequence described on page 104. The first picture shows the speedometer and brake system—the background image that didn't change. Next you see the car frame, which moved up and down, and then the speedometer needle, which moved around the dial. Finally, the composite image shows how the audience saw the sequence when all three slides were projected. The sequence required dozens of slides and twelve projectors, and even then the movement wasn't smooth enough. As noted in the text, this problem was resolved in the post-production phase, with an ADO.

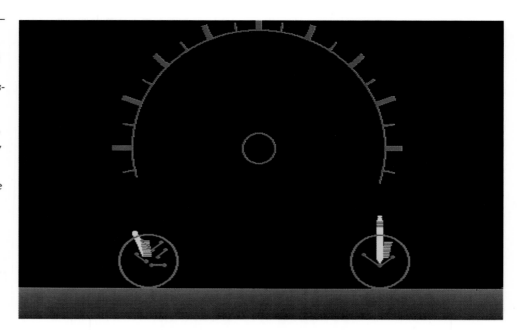

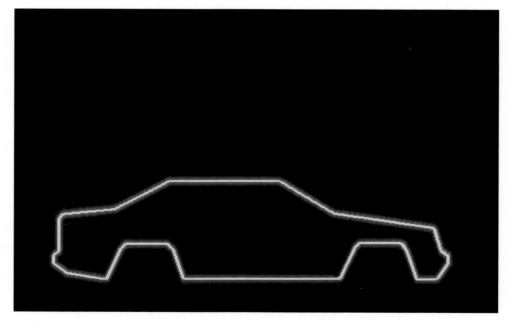

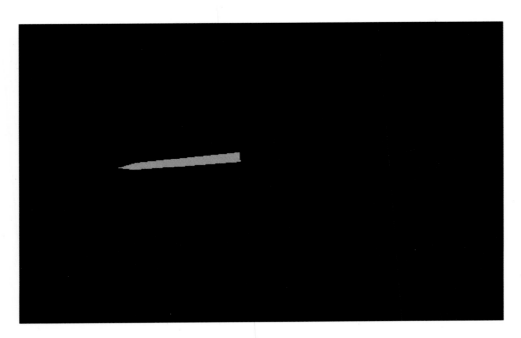

This sequence involves the animation of a helicopter. Only one helicopter was painted on the computer. It was then copied, reduced in different proportions, and repositioned on the screen. Separate slides were then made of each image, and they were projected from a series of projectors—all computer-controlled to get the timing right. To the audience it looks as if the helicopter were flying toward them.

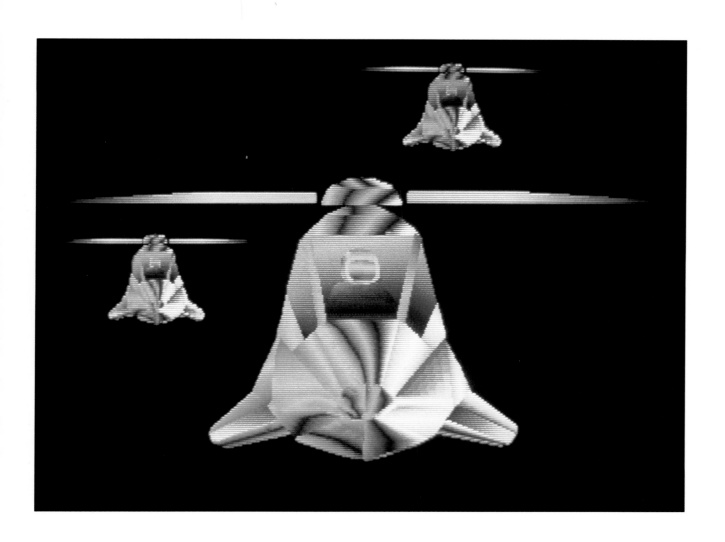

ANIMATING WITH COLOR CYCLING

A different way of producing animation is by using the color-cycling function and recording directly onto videotape. A friend of mine refers to this function as "chasing lights," likening it to a movie marquee. In any case it is a capability peculiar to paint software with a palette of 256 colors at any one time (chosen from 16.7 million).

Admittedly, cycle animation is limited in its effects, but it is often exactly what clients need for a striking audiovisual presentation (using videotape). Take a simple growth chart as an example. In slide form it appears static and bland. Think of how much more attention it will attract if it is animated.

Before computer graphics, doing even a simple animation, such as moving a red line upward on a growth chart, would have required the time-consuming and expensive process of cel animation. With this traditional cel method, a three-second animation would require 90 individual frames (30 per sec-

ond). In other words, a single-frame video recorder would have to record 90 individual pictures to create a red line that moves smoothly across the screen in three seconds. That's a lot of cels to paint by hand.

Now what happens with cycle animation? First you create the necessary palette. In this case you need 90 color changes, so you will need 180 spaces on your palette: 90 to hold the fill color (red) and 90 to hold the background color. When you're setting up the animation, however, it's best to make slots #91–180 on your palette multicolored. Later, before you start the color cycling, you can convert these slots to a solid background color (black, for instance).

On your screen you now set up the growth line on a grid with 90 vertical slices. Each of the slices within the line must be filled with a different palette color (from #91 to #180), proceeding sequentially by number from left to right. That's why you want this part of your palette multicolored to begin

with—so it's easy to keep track of your progression.

After all the slices are filled in and you've changed colors #91–180 to the background color (black), you're ready to begin the color cycling. The color cycle is set for palette squares #1–180 at a speed of three seconds. In the example here (shown on the facing page), the colors cycle from left to right—but this could easily be reversed. What happens is that, as the cycle begins, the red colors from #1 through #90 flow, one by one, into squares #91 through #180, gradually filling all the thin slices until the entire line is red. If you let the cycle continue, the black background color would reappear at the lower left and the process of filling in would repeat.

The cycling process can be put onto 1-inch, ¾-inch, or ½-inch videotape through the use of a genlock module and NTSC encoder. The recording is made in real time—three seconds. Contrast this to the time needed to create art in traditional cel animation.

To animate this growth chart, I first set up my palette, with colors #1–90 red and #91–180 each a distinct tone. Then I filled in the sections of the growth line, starting with color #91 and proceeding in order through #180. After changing colors #91–180 to black, I began cycling colors #1–90, so that color #90 first replaced #91, then #92, and so on "up" the line. Actually, this was a rather complicated way of doing this chart. Instead of filling in each slice initially, you could simply create a shaded rectangle from color #91 on one side to color #180 on the other (using the process described on page 46), draw the line, and erase the rest. You'd then be ready to start the color-cycling process.

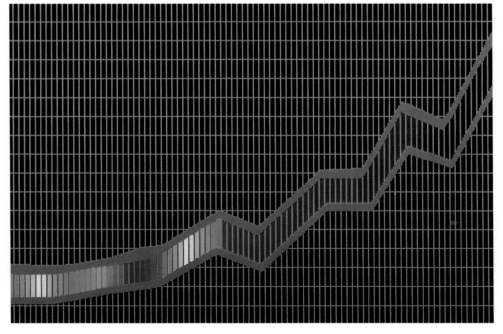

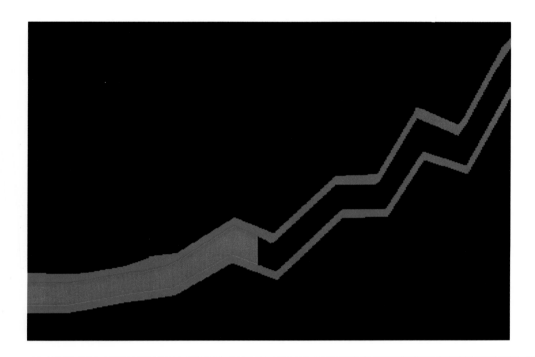

Of course, there are many times when the animation is more complicated than color cycling allows. But it's a useful technique to remember, especially if you're working on a tight budget. Look back, for example, at the illustrations for *Maxx Trax II*. On page 93 the laser beam can be animated with color cycling, increasing the explosive impact. Or, on page 95, the columns can be animated, making them rotate. The control panel be-

hind the two vehicles on page 95 offers another example. It was designed so that all four colors can cycle, giving the impression of great electronic activity.

All these examples deal with moving one color at a time through a defined area. But groups of colors can also be moved. Look, for example, at the cone on page 114, which seems to tumble through space when all nine of its colors cycle at the same time.

Cycle animation may be the humblest form of computer animation, but some of its products will be around for a long time. Just ask a TV producer how most weather maps are created. That jet stream zooming down from Canada into the Great Plains—that's a color cycle. So are all those pulsing weather fronts, snowflakes, and raindrops. Color cycling is quick and economical. Even more—a definite bonus—it's fun.

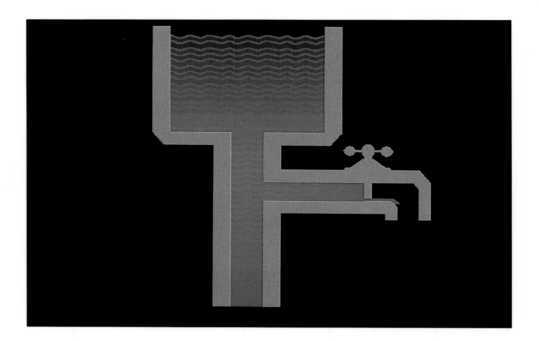

This simple but effective use of color cycling describes the flow of water through a leaky faucet. Any circulating system—be it plumbing, electricity, or the body's own circulatory system—is an ideal subject for color-cycle animation. Here the sequence begins with a full tank of water. The water (color) then leaks out in three drops—running from one drop to the next (only the first and last are shown here). The principle is essentially the same as for the red growth line on the previous page.

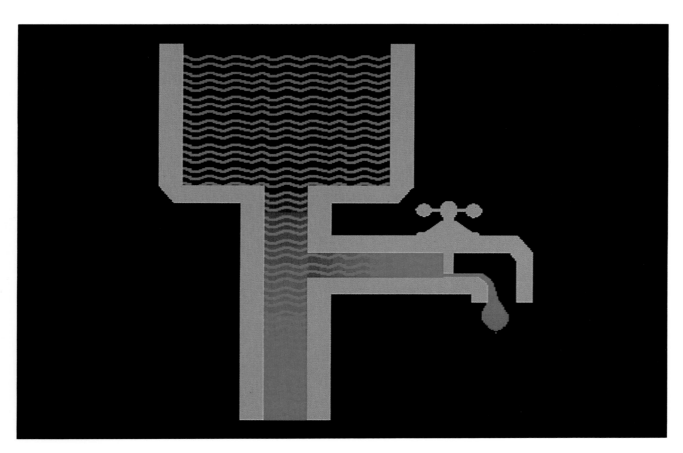

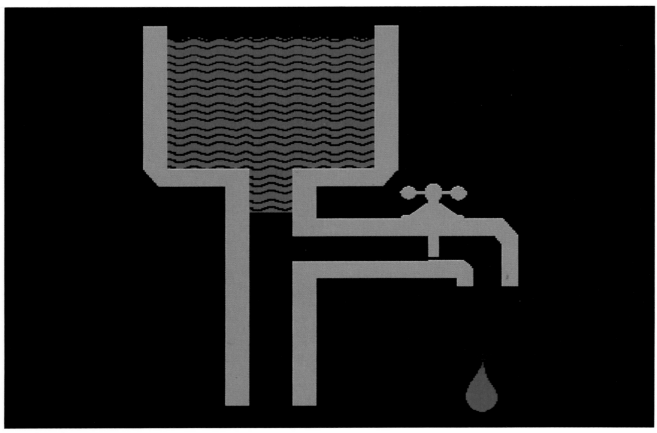

Here you can see how it's possible to show an object moving through space with color-cycle animation. The first image shows you the complete drawing and the full color palette (done in black and white here to simplify matters). Each truncated cone is made up of nine colors, with its own distinct place on the color palette. If, instead of moving one color at a time, you now move nine colors at once—keeping the rest of the palette black—first one cone and then the next will become visible. Remember that you see only one cone at a time. Thus, if the cycle speed is fast enough, the same cone seems to fly forward in a spiral toward you. Note that it was only necessary to create one cone here. All the others could be made by copying, enlarging, and rotating the first.

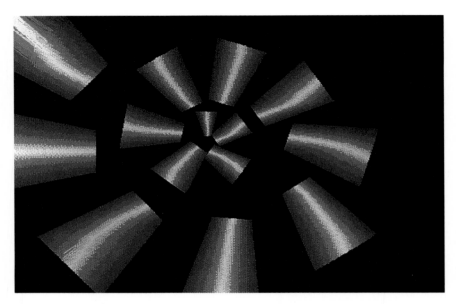

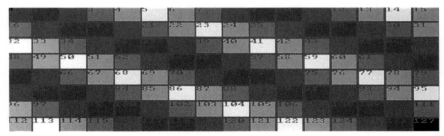

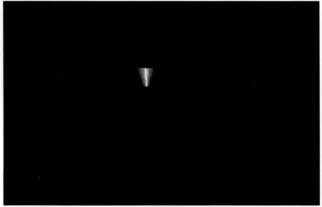

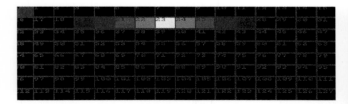

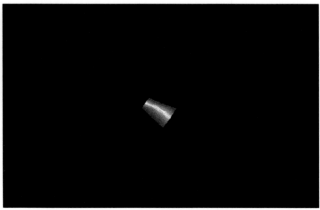

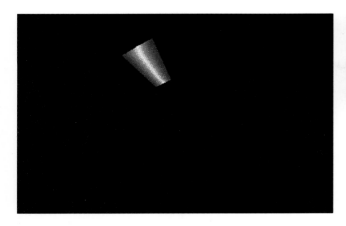
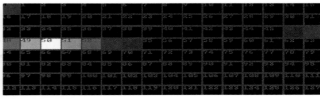
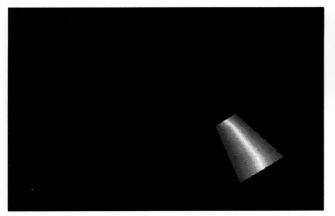
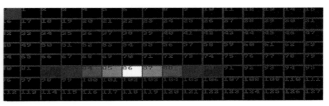
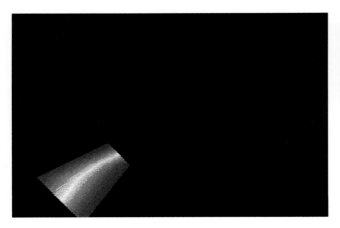

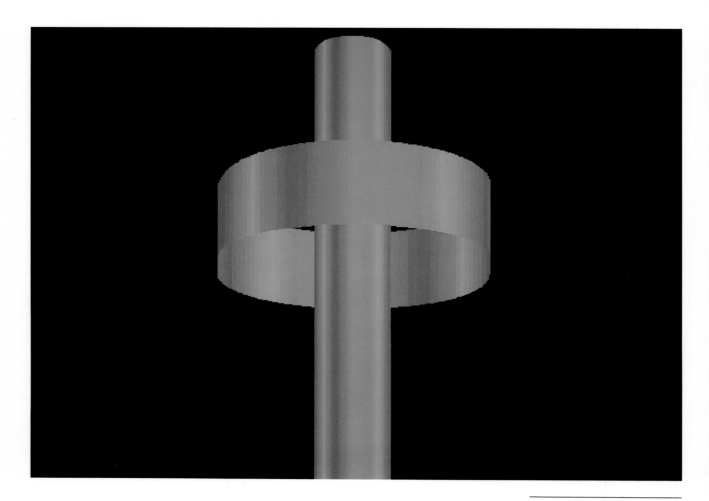

This machine-like form can also be easily animated with color cycling. If you look closely at the circular form, you can see the different color "slices." As the palette moves through these slices, this part will seem to revolve around the central cylinder.

*This weather map repre-
sents a popular use of color-
cycle animation. Not only
does the air seem to circu-
late within the front, but the
snowflakes pulsate and the
raindrops flicker, as if they
were falling. What's really
moving here is the color.*

PART THREE

THREE-DIMENSIONAL PROGRAMS

MEMO
12/5   7:45 A.M.

From: R. T. Stonewall, President
         One Stop Computers, Inc.
To: M. R. Jackson, Account Executive
         Smart Guys Advertising, Inc.
Re: Push for three-dimensional
         capabilities

We've finally done it. We've added a math co-processor, more memory, a larger hard disk, and a 32-bit graphics board. What does that mean? It means that now our new three-dimensional design software can take those two-dimensional, desk-bound artists to places "they've never been before." OK, Ms. Jackson, put your engines in Warp 9.

MEMO
12/5   4:30 P.M.

From: M. R. Jackson, Account Executive
         Smart Guys Advertising, Inc.
To: R. T. Stonewall, President
         One Stop Computers, Inc.

How's this, R. T.? We've put your new software to use and "drawn" the real, three-dimensional figure out of a flat, two-dimensional silhouette. Of course, the sequence will be animated, with a lively tune for the jingle attached. Hope you like it.

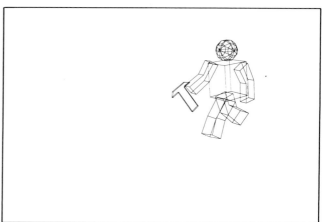
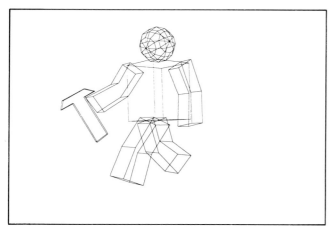

(SCRIPT)

Has your life gone dull and flat?
Is everything just a silhouette?
One Stop can change all that . . .
Come to us and see what you get!

We'll give you a fully rounded base,
Add a new dimension to your day,
Get you up and going and moving in space—
The 3-D One Stop Computer way.

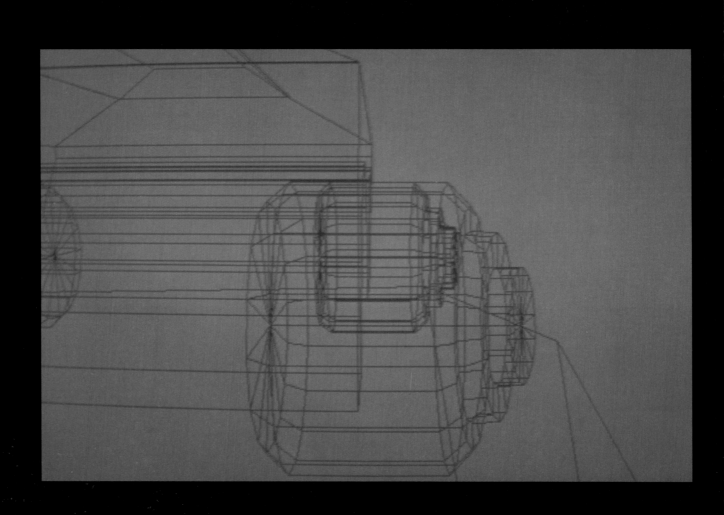

SPATIAL DRAWING

This may be the age of supersonic jets and orbiting spacecraft, but a friend confessed recently that none of these high-tech achievements excited him as much as watching an ultralight flying machine slowly circle his house. His statement comes as no surprise: from mythic times people have wanted wings. The evidence is in our language and our art. Being unable to fly on our own power, we settle for flights of imagination.

For the graphic artist, a major challenge for the imagination has always been the rendering of three dimensions in two dimensions. But now there is a new computer tool that makes this transformation all the easier. Three-dimensional design programs offer an advance on two-dimensional systems, replacing the traditional pencil lines that suggest space with a wireframe construction that encloses space. This construction can be seen from any angle; it can even be entered or encircled—it is a true three-dimensional model.

Three-dimensional computer sketches provide almost unlimited spatial freedom for the imagination. Not only can you see the form in space, you can also modify the form and the space it is in. This last aspect gives wings to the artist. Just as the ultralight flying machine carries its pilot over treetops in slowly circling maneuvers, so, too, does the three-dimensional graphics program guide its user over, around, and through the microworld of artistic creation.

This image was taken directly off the computer screen, to give you an idea of what the three-dimensional drawing looks like while you're doing it. The car shown is one of the many views done for the sequence described on page 134.

CREATING VOLUME

An artist draws a square on a piece of paper. A few more lines drawn in perspective, and the square becomes a cube. If a little tone is added and perhaps a shadow at the base of the cube, the illusion of a volume in space is quickly and effectively created. This is the traditional way of picturing a form in space.

Using a three-dimensional design program, you begin the same way, by drawing a square on the screen. But there the similarity ends. From this point on, space is represented, not by shadows or shading, but by lines rendered with the computer's help. Amazingly, the computer does most of the work, conducting its business in private, depending on the artist only to give it the right directions. And, fortunately for those traditional artists lacking a lot of computer knowledge, the necessary commands and pro-

cedures are easy to understand.

For three-dimensional programs, the drawing instrument is often a mouse—not quite a pencil, but a tool that soon becomes just as much a part of the artist. The drawing surface—the screen—actually presents two views of the work in progress. One is the plane view, on which each of the three dimensions (x, y, and z) can be seen in a flat contour form, much as in an architectural elevation. The other view is a three-dimensional, perspective view, showing all three planes at the same time. The actual drawing is usually done when the screen is in the plane, or flat, mode.

But let's return to our example. How does the cube follow the square? With this question we enter into a fundamental difference between two-dimensional and three-dimensional modeling. Simply stated, the difference is that

two-dimensional modeling deals with the illusion of space, while three-dimensional modeling creates actual space.

Our initial square is drawn in contour on the x plane. This square becomes a cube simply by commanding the computer to extrude the square a distance equal to one of its sides. The extrusion occurs in a direction at right angles to the plane on which the square is drawn. After the computer completes the extrusion (almost instantaneously), you just switch the screen to the perspective mode—and there is the cube. It is transparent and spindly, not nearly as substantial in looks as its traditionally drawn cousin. But don't be deceived by its looks. It behaves as if it had actual volume, not merely the illusion of it. If, for instance, you change its position in space, its configuration will change appropriately. But more on that later.

For three-dimensional programs the drawing tool is often a mouse, rather than the stylus used with two-dimensional software. Here, using a three-dimensional program, the mouse is shown from different angles. Keep in mind that only one drawing was done to get all these views.

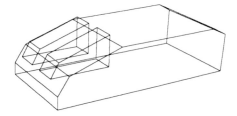

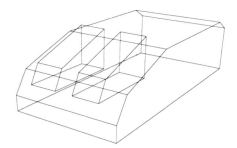

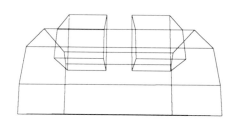

This drawing of a cube was done with a two-dimensional program, using traditional perspective and shading techniques. In other words, to transform the square into a cube, I had to actually draw the lines (or at least indicate their endpoints). The modeling then heightens the illusion of volume. Note that I could have drawn this cube in traditional media, with pencil on paper, but using the two-dimensional software dramatizes the difference between two- and three-dimensional computer graphics.

With a three-dimensional program, the computer takes care of all the perspective drawing. After drawing the initial square, you just instruct the computer to extrude it a distance equal to one of the sides. The resulting cube has "real" dimension, in that the computer will alter its perspective appropriately when you shift its position on the screen. The cube actually turns in space, reforming itself in the new position. Another instance of computer magic.

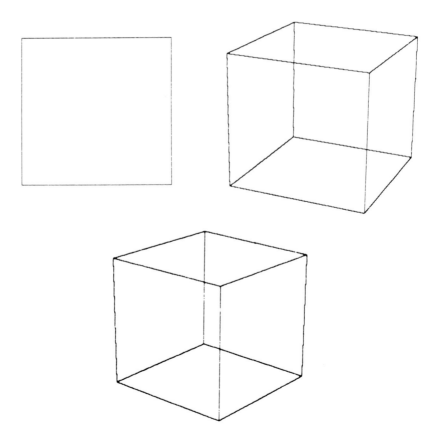

EXTRUDING AND SWEEPING

The extrusion procedure used for the cube on the preceding page is fundamental to three-dimensional design programs. All kinds of shapes can be transformed into three-dimensional objects with this technique. Consider, for example, a wheel. As with the cube, the place to begin is with a simple two-dimensional shape—in this case a circle. This circle is then outlined on either the x, y, or z plane, just as the square was. The next step is to tell the computer how fat you want the wheel to be and ask it to extrude the circle. The extruded wheel may look like a slice of a cylinder, or perhaps a thin bracelet, but it has a three-dimensional reality.

So far we've dealt with relatively simple shapes. But what if you want a tire rather than a wheel? Can extrusion be used to create a fully delineated tire, with tread and thick and thin sections? To make such complex curved forms, three-dimensional programs use a procedure called "sweep." It works this way: instead of drawing a circle to begin with, you draw the contour of a cross-section of the tire. The three-dimensional program then sweeps the outer edge completely around an axis—in this case the opposite edge at the hub of the tire. The sweep routine can go from 1 to 360 degrees, making a tire, an apple, or even an apple with a missing slice.

Obviously these procedures save the designer an incredible amount of time, besides eliminating the tedium of perspective drawing. Even more, they can fuel the artist's imagination. Using the sweep function on an irregular doodle shape, for example, can lead to some wonderful surprises (see page 126). You may even find some likely candidates for science-fiction illustrations.

And keep in mind that all these shapes—mundane and fantastic alike—can be changed. Individual lines can be moved; so can points. When that happens, the entire shape changes to conform to the new position. Take a look at the nose on the helmet on page 127, as it becomes longer—and then longer.

Many other transformations are possible. As with two-dimensional programs, shapes can be copied, enlarged, or reduced. It's also possible to zoom in, enlarging an area so it is easier to select the lines and points you want to manipulate. The possibilities for transformation, especially with more complicated forms, seem endless.

From the two-dimensional drawing of a slice of an apple it is possible to create a fully three-dimensional form by using the sweep capabilities of the three-dimensional programs. As you can see, you can stop the sweep at any point, so that it looks as if part of the apple had been cut away.

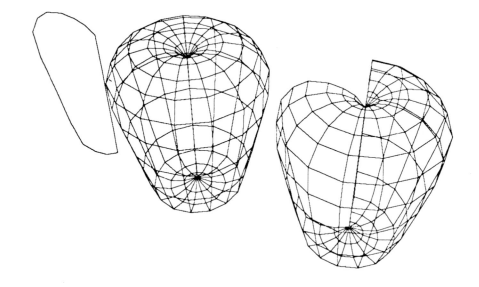

Nothing is simpler than a circle—especially when you don't have to draw it. A couple of clicks of the mouse is about all you need to get a basic circle on a three-dimensional program. After that it's just a matter of having the computer extrude the circle into a wheel or cylinder. These steps will also give you a lampshade, like the one on pages 130–131.

ORIGINAL DRAWING

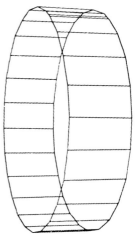

COMPUTER-GENERATED
PERSPECTIVE VIEW

All that was drawn for this tire was the simple outline of the tire's cross-section on the top left. This was then "swept" by the computer to create the complex three-dimensional form. (The other plane views were also generated by the computer.) This tire is a good example of how an artist trained to think in two-dimensional terms might begin to change his or her visual thinking.

ORIGINAL DRAWING

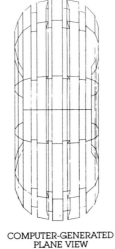

COMPUTER-GENERATED
PLANE VIEW

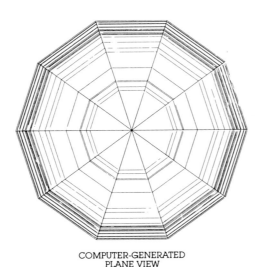

COMPUTER-GENERATED
PLANE VIEW

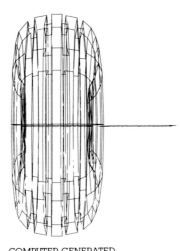

COMPUTER-GENERATED
PERSPECTIVE VIEW

EXTRUDING AND SWEEPING

Artists doodle all the time; for some, it's a crucial part of the creative process. What happens if the sweep routine is used on a doodle? Quite simply—the unexpected! Of course, not every doodle is worth saving, but every now and then there is that lucky accident. And it doesn't take long for artists to incorporate such lucky accidents into a larger scheme.

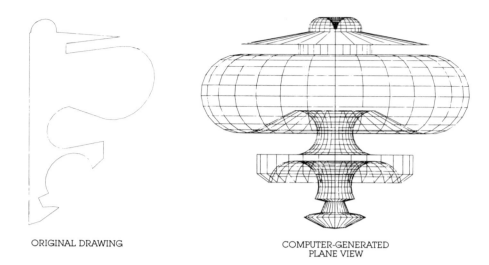

ORIGINAL DRAWING

COMPUTER-GENERATED
PLANE VIEW

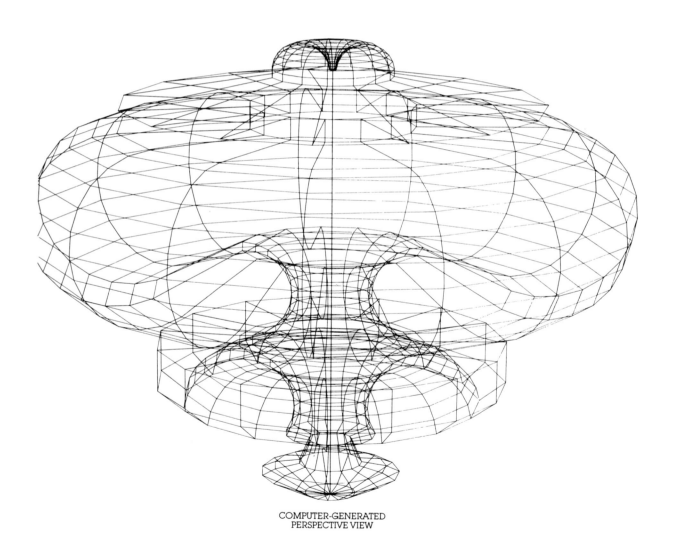

COMPUTER-GENERATED
PERSPECTIVE VIEW

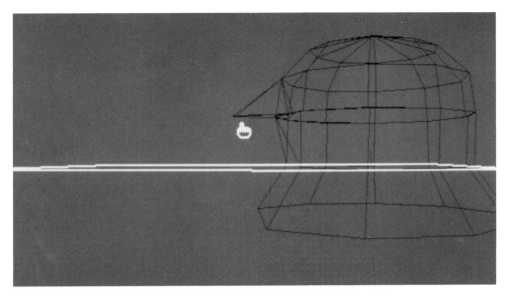

The flexibility of the computer encourages playful exploration with three-dimensional programs just as much as with two-dimensional ones. In this case I decided to play with the nose on the helmet, elongating it by literally pulling on the tip. Actually the wireframe model can be manipulated in many ways. In some cases, as with the nose, the artist "manually" drags points or edges to new positions. But the artist can also command the computer to move entire figures automatically, simply by typing in the distance—for example, "move the sofa six feet two inches to the left."

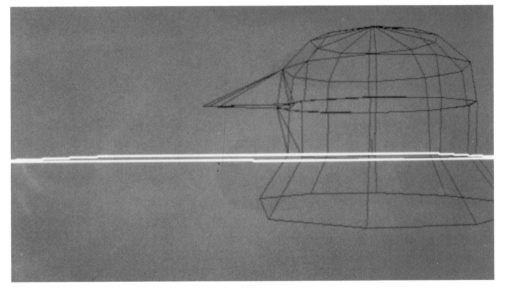

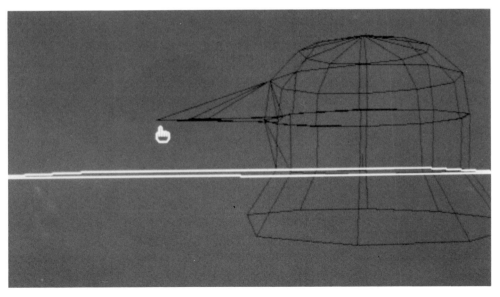

TRAVELING THROUGH SPACE

This chapter began with a discussion of the ever-present human wish to fly. In a very real sense, three-dimensional design programs enable you to fly—or at least travel—through the world you have created on your computer screen. Using simple extrusions of various-size rectangles, you can set up an environment like the town square shown on the facing page and then move through that environment, zooming in over the buildings and circling around for a closer look.

Capturing a sensation of space has always been a challenge for the artist. It has been said that a playwright must pay as much attention to the stage positions of the characters as to the words they speak—imagining the spatial configuration while writing the dialogue. In a similar way, the artist must be aware of the relationships between forms in space while working on the actual rendering of the forms. Consider the following: in your mind's eye, you conceive an interior—a plain, all-white room, with four walls, a floor, and a ceiling. A chair appears, then a table. At first you put the chair against the rear wall and the table in the center of the room. But then you begin to wonder: Should the table perhaps be next to the chair? As more and more furniture is added, your imagination becomes more and more crowded, so it is difficult to remember the entire room. The answer to this dilemma is the sketch. Sketches work as shorthand notes from the imagination, offering you tangible proof of your idea while freeing your imagination to go on to new visions.

But what does all this have to do with computer graphics? With a three-dimensional program you can enter your imaginary room and move around it, viewing the objects from every direction. You don't have to redraw the sketch each time. Instead, you can zoom in for a closer look or rotate the room for a different perspective.

After working with three-dimensional programs for a while, you may find that your imaginative process has changed. Objects and their surroundings appear less as profiles and patterns, and more as complete worlds . . . worlds with hidden sides and interior spaces . . . worlds within their own universe.

The computer allows you to zoom in from the distance on this town square; then shift direction, circling over the buildings as you move in closer to the clocktower. You can even go behind the clocktower and look out at the square from the opposite direction, as shown in the last picture here.

As with the town square on the preceding page, it's possible to move in closer and closer on this room, enter through the door, approach the chair near the far wall, and then sit down and look back toward the lamp. Here the objects are all shown in the transparent, wireframe mode, because it's easiest to do your sketching and manipulations in that mode. But you can fill in the frames to give the picture a fully modeled look. You might, for example, want to block in the wall in the second image to clarify what you would see through the open door.

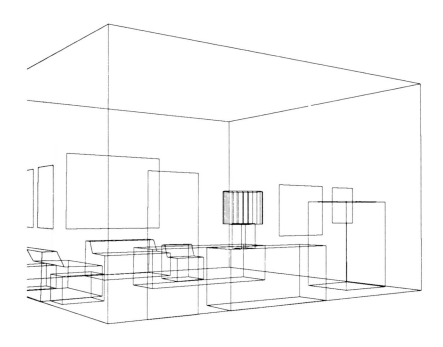

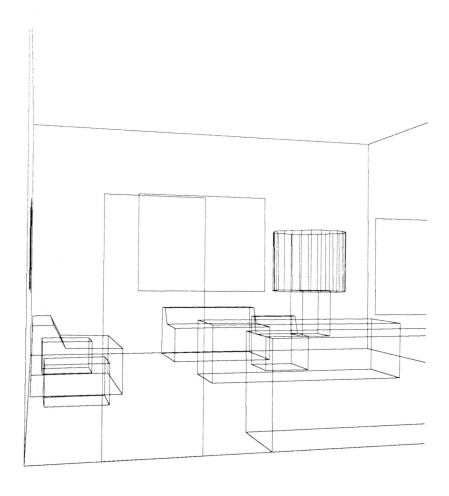

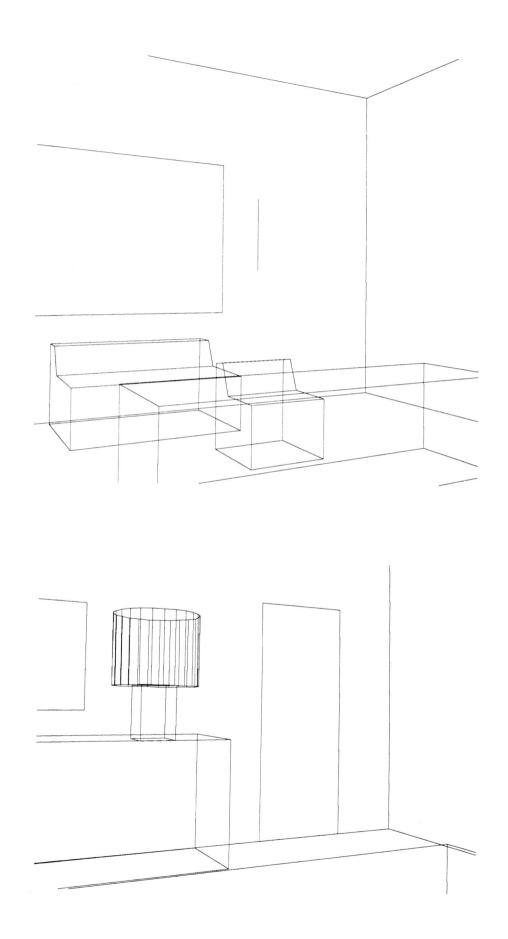

THE COMPUTER AS CAMERA

Movies have changed the way we look at the world. The camera, reflecting the aspirations of its operator, has become airborne. On the screen we now look through the eyes of a hawk, zoom in and out, pan around, up, and down. Much of this freedom is due to superior technology, but it was the imaginative moviemakers who forced the technology to accommodate their expansive vision.

The art director sitting at a drawing board, roughing out a storyboard for a live-action ad, is a descendant of the great moviemakers. And, though the art director's body may be confined to a desk, his or her imagination is not. But there is a limitation: often the ability to express the ideas of a plastic, kinetic imagination is restricted to static, two-dimensional media. The result is a gap between what comes to mind and what can be conveyed on paper with felt-tip markers. Much of the designer's creative authority is, by default, handed over to the film production company.

Some art directors try to overcome this by being at the actual shoot, but they rarely have any impact. Usually they must defer to the film director's expertise. What art directors need is a visualizing tool that employs the same spatial and kinetic language as film—a desktop filmmaker. Three-dimensional design programs offer that possibility. An art director can create a microworld that is a scaled-down version of real space and then move through it, ending up with precise directions for the shoot or even a sample videotape.

This illustration was done several years ago by Joe Cychosz and Dave Plunkett on the Control Data Cyber 205, a supercomputer at the Purdue CAD Lab. Today desktop equipment can provide many of the three-dimensional color-modeling capabilities you see here.

DOING A COMPUTER STORYBOARD

How does the computer work as a desktop filmmaker? Consider a hypothetical ad for a newly designed all-terrain car, which can go anywhere. To dramatize this selling point, the client wants the car shown in the middle of a desert—on top of a small mesa. (Actually I saw an ad along these lines once on TV.)

It is a fantastic opportunity for camera angles. Think about zooming in from a distance and doing a complete circle around the car, or doing a series of shots from below, rapidly climbing to just above the hood. The alternatives seem endless, although not all are equally effective.

The first step, of course, is to create the car. It doesn't have to be a detailed version of the real thing, just enough to convey the feeling of the original. Using the extrusion and sweep functions, among others, you can create a wireframe model. Then perch it on the edge of the mesa—a nice dramatic touch, and one that allows the front end to be viewed from below.

Now you are ready to play with different perspectives and angles, getting the computer's "eye" to move around the model. Instead of a deskbound artist, you've become a desktop filmmaker—trying one view, then another; changing angles at will. Once you decide on a beginning, middle, and end for a sequence, you can instruct the computer to complete the move in four, eight, or twenty frames. (Note that when the computer plays the sequence a greater number of frames will create a smoother but slower move, while fewer frames will result in a jumpier but faster transition.)

The sequence on the facing page represents only one of many possibilities for this hypothetical ad. But just think of the work and time that would be involved in presenting these options in the conventional two-dimensional sto-ryboard format. Granted, the wire-frame drawings do not have the same quality as a fully rendered marker comp. But you can print each computer view and then color it with traditional techniques for presentation purposes. Or, even better, you can use the computer itself to render the wireframe structures as solid models (see pages 138–139) and then output them as slides using a film recorder. Yet another possibility, of course, is to playback the sequence on the monitor itself, so the client and—even more important—the film producer can see the action. Then you can give the producer a simple printout of the sequence, to use as a guide for the shots and setups.

None of the images just mentioned are meant to be used as finished art. Often three-dimensional design programs are used to create working scripts that serve as guides to the actual filming. That's mainly because most TV ad work is live action. But if an ad called for the animation of computer-generated imagery in solid form, three-dimensional programs could provide the finished work.

To animate a five-second move around the car shown here, for example, you would need 30 frames, or views, of the car per second—or 150 separate views for five seconds. The views themselves are no problem; the complexity comes with creating fully colored versions of these views. Fortunately, there are now programs that incorporate two-dimensional paint effects (known as texture mapping) with three-dimensional modeling software. At the moment it takes a while for the desktop computer to do this, but the technology is rapidly improving. And if the past is any guide to the future, there will soon be a lot of artists and designers doing their own computer-generated imagery for animation.

This wireframe sequence exemplifies what I would call a three-dimensional storyboard. Here twelve views are enough to convey the sense of a camera moving around the subject—but, of course, there could have been more. If all the lines seem confusing, note that there are programs that will remove the lines the eye would not ordinarily see (called "hidden-line removal"). The end result would then resemble a more traditionally done line drawing. Another benefit of hidden-line removal is reduced strain on the laser printer (the kind of printer used here), which has difficulty handling a lot of lines and polygons.

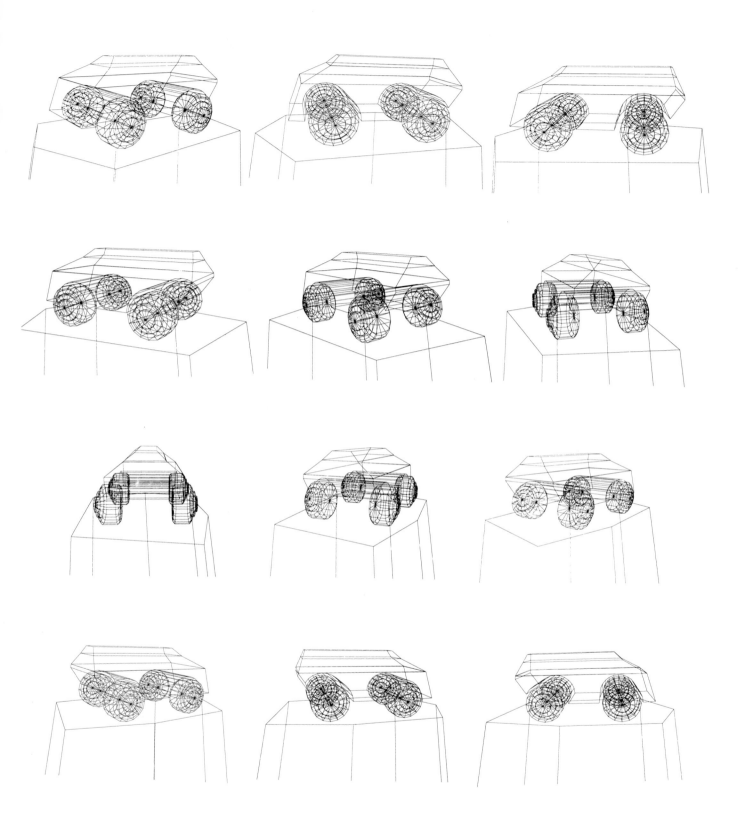

This sequence is related to the one on the preceding page, but here the forms have been completely modeled, giving them a much more solid look. Also note that now there is a definite light source. This light source can be changed—allowing for even more experimentation before any filming takes place. Although the image is shown in black-and-white here, different colors could also be tried for different effects. Obviously, it's a tremendous advantage to be able to test all these possibilities before you begin shooting an ad.

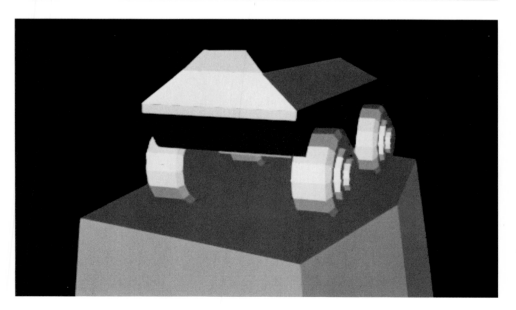

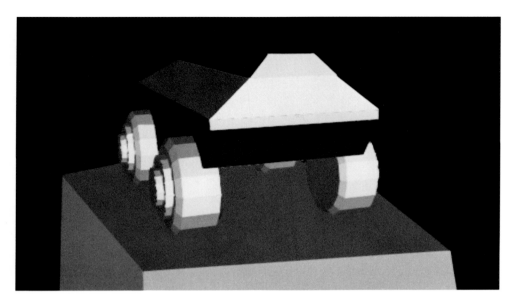

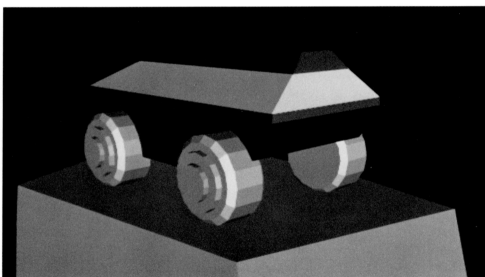

CONCLUSION

We have always been tool-makers. Indeed, human prehistory is illuminated in great measure by the discovery of primitive tools. Anthropologists use tools to measure a society's achievement; the better and more sophisticated the tools, the more advanced, technologically, the society.

It is no surprise, then, to find that contemporary society puts great store in its ability to invent newer and cleverer gadgets. "Build a better mousetrap and the world will beat a path to your door" succinctly expresses the value that modern society attaches to "improved" technology; landing a man on the moon being merely a high-tech variant of the same theme.

Tool-making is a manifestation of the human imagination, just as the creation of art is. It is even fair to assume that some of the earliest tools were developed explicitly to make art. Imagine the scene deep in the caves of Altamira some 20,000 years ago: the artist comtemplates the bare torchlit wall of the cave; on the ground, ready for use, lies an array of painting and drawing tools (charred sticks, large and small animal hair brushes, piles of colored pigment, bowls of liquid). Everything, however, is on hold until the artist decides on the all-important first stroke.

Today, 20,000 years later, the computer graphics artist is faced with the same situation. An electronic stylus has replaced the charred stick and pixels have displaced powdered pigment, but the rest of the creative act remains unchanged.

So, does it matter that computer graphics keeps expanding its range of functions while becoming easier to use? If greater power brings broader responsibilities, then perhaps the question is not, "Where is computer graphics going?" but, "What are artists doing to prepare themselves to use it?"

The cave drawings testify to the abilities of their creators to observe reality, interpret that reality, and render those interpretations in stylistically compelling images. But it is only the last step that deals with materials and techniques. It is the first two—observation and interpretation—that set apart those members of society called artists. These are skills that must be practiced and perfected with computer technology, as well as traditional methods. If five or ten years from now, a computer graphics workstation appears that will allow a single artist in the privacy of his or her studio to conceive, design, and execute a fully animated, three-dimensional video with color, movable light sources, realistic textures—and then to design and illustrate a full-color brochure, complete with type, to accompany that video—the artist will have to be ready for it. Who knows, perhaps computer graphics will be instrumental in reviving the concept of the Renaissance man—producing a latter-day da Vinci, an artist well-grounded in the fundamentals of art but curious about techniques and willing to abandon the security of established methods for the adventure of exploring the new.

The only sure answer is that computer technologies will continue to grow, putting more graphic power, at lower cost, into the hands of those artists who want it. And because computer graphics is electronic, it will be a global medium, available almost instantly anyplace. It will hasten the development of a global, language-independent, visual vocabulary. As the design and illustration component of video, computer graphics will surpass its print counterpart as the most ubiquitous format for the display of images. Businesses and other establishments, which have relied on the printed word, will succumb to the growing appetite for graphics.

All these developments (and many are already underway) will create a greater demand for visually sophisticated people. It is an ironic twist for those who, at the introduction of computer graphics, feared that it would put artists out of work. On the contrary, the electronic revolution in art is just beginning.

APPENDIX: GETTING STARTED

One of the first steps you may want to take is to learn how to operate a computer graphics system. Most large cities have at least several schools that provide training in computer graphics. Outside of the large cities, there are colleges and even high schools that offer adult-education courses in computers. They also, from time to time, feature workshops, seminars, and lectures on special topics like computer graphics. If you can find a workshop that provides hands-on instruction, that's the best bet. Professional organizations, such as local chapters of the Graphic Artists Guild, and art directors clubs also offer workshops and lectures on current technological developments in the art field.

Beyond basic education, there's the question of whether you want to invest in a computer graphics system of your own. The rapid growth and development of computer graphics make accurate predictions about its future difficult. These factors also create uncertainty in recommending specific paint systems. As this is being written, for example, a well-known supplier of computer graphics workstations has just been purchased and its products folded into the new owner's line. The old name is gone, and a potential buyer looking for products under that label will be lost. This is not an isolated event, nor the last, in a field where buyouts have become a fact of business.

So how, if you want to make a purchase, do you get enough information to make an intelligent choice? The same advice applies to individual artists, studios, ad agencies, and corporate design departments. But note that if you are an artist or designer in the corporate arena, you must make a special effort to be included in the decision-making loop. Too often major purchases, such as computer graphics workstations, are controlled by management people who know nothing about the nitty-gritty of design and are too accepting of the pitch delivered by fast-talking salespeople. Management's role should be confined to the economic end; let the artist be the judge of a system's applicability.

But how do you become a knowledgeable judge? The first step is to find out what's out there. Five or six years ago that would have meant learning about a handful of companies. Today, however, there are so many that going through all of them would give you a terminal case of option shock. But take heart: there is something you can do, which you

---

The development of this image reflects some of the basic capabilities of the computer. The artist—Elaine Raphael—began with a single flower; next she reduced it and tacked it on—in reverse—to the larger flower, which she then mirrored. She continued to mirror the image—top to bottom and side to side—until she arrived at the final pattern on the lower right.

are already expert at, that will make your job easier. Begin with a long, hard, objective look at the work you do now and the clients who use it. Chances are that 80 to 85 percent of that work is repeat business from a stable client-base. Now select a representative sampling of your work—use this as a standard to sort out those computer graphics systems that fit your needs and those that don't.

With this partial protection from option shock, you're ready to take a thorough look at the current literature on computer graphics, especially magazines. Pay particular attention to listings of new products (as well as ads for established systems). Also keep an eye out for upcoming computer shows. Write or call for information on anything that interests you.

Computer shows are convenient forums for seeing similar systems in operation, and they can be an excellent source of information if you follow a few simple guidelines. Most important, go with a sample of your work and show it to the salesperson of any system that intrigues you. If this sounds obvious, keep in mind that computer graphics workstations are neither simple nor straightforward. Shopping for a computer graphics system is not like going to an art supply store for a brush—a computer graphics system *is* an art supply store. By adhering to your specific demands, you'll avoid adding to the legion of computer graphics systems that sit unused, gathering dust.

But beware: presenting a salesperson with definite requirements doesn't always work. Not only do computers do many things, they also promise a lot. Salespeople are adept at parrying your specific request with an offer of future fulfillment. "In three months we'll be able to do that" is a typical line; indeed, it's such an endemic problem that the industry has coined a word to describe it—"vaporware." To avoid this pitfall, insist on a

demonstration of the current software.

Keep in mind that exhibitors at computer shows usually have prepared demos—"canned" routines on disk or videotape that show off the software. They're great for displaying the product but give no clue about the process. For that, you must see the system create something original. No reputable exhibitor with confidence in the company's product should refuse a reasonable request for a live demo; I would have serious doubts about any company that did refuse.

The next guideline covers the system's actual cost. If system *x* passes the first two tests—it produces what your clients like and can be operated by a nontechnical artist—then evaluate the following factors to determine if it's affordable:

- *Cost of finished art.* In addition to the cost of the system itself, figure in the cost of any input device (such as a scanner) and output device (printer, film recorder, video encoder, or tape recorder) necessary to produce finished art that you can deliver to your client.
- *Training.* Some vendors include training in their selling price, but others add it on. Determine whether this is group training or one-on-one; also ask at whose facility the training takes place.
- *Finance and service costs.* Find out about finance or leasing charges, as well as service and maintenance contracts. The latter usually include upgrades of software—a must if you are to remain competitive.
- *Operator learning curve.* Beyond the initial training, you must factor in the time it takes for all operators to become relatively proficient. Estimating this depends on several variables: the complexity of the system, the individual talents of the trainees, and the number of trainees.

Salespeople, when asked about this cost, tend to downplay the time needed to be productive. To be on the safe side, double their estimates.

- *Client learning curve.* Although I've never seen this issue addressed, client understanding of the computer graphics product is almost as important as your understanding of it. Many clients, particularly in the print area, are unaware of the possibilities of computer graphics. Introducing them to new methods requires extra time and attention—a definite cost, but one that's difficult to estimate. A good rule of thumb is to add 10 to 15 percent of the normal time a job takes for client education.

In addition to talking to the salespeople and reading through the brochures, try to make contact with some of the other people attending the show. Many are computer enthusiasts, and they can provide a wealth of information on everything from software performance (bugs and all) to a list of suppliers who do (or do not) support their customers.

If attending shows is impractical, contact the vendors of those systems which interest you (based on information in magazines or brochures). Often, you'll be given a chance to have a hands-on demonstration at a nearby dealer's showroom. Some companies have traveling sales shows and are happy to schedule appointments for in-depth demonstrations of their systems.

For "inside" information, check out some of the users' groups—organizations of people who use specific computer systems. Though their information may be too narrowly focused for an overview, they can be helpful in providing advice on specific programs and hardware.

Once you've decided on the kind of system you need and established the cost, you might ask the vendor to place the system at your site for a test period—thirty to ninety days, depending on the system's complexity. Although this request is not popular, my experience as a consultant suggests that to buy without this kind of subjective evaluation can be an invitation to aggravation (at best) or economic disaster (at worst).

If you run into a stone wall in requesting on-site evaluations, then demand that at least one or two of your typical projects be done on the seller's demonstration system—with you in attendance while the job is being done. If you're told that's not possible, I would seriously suggest you look elsewhere.

Of course, all the suggestions I've given take time. If your current commitments make this investment of time impractical, then your only recourse is to hire a consultant. In addition to experience with computer systems, a computer graphics consultant should have a working knowledge of your graphic design business. And make sure he or she knows exactly what you want the system to do. To reiterate my earlier advice: the best expert on what you do is you. Using that as the starting and the focal point will save everyone concerned time, money, and aggravation.

INDEX